Amanda Knox

For
Mum and Dad
My personal cheerleaders Susan and Andy
My brilliant children
And Mark, who made it possible for me to write this book

Amanda Knox

Crime, Trial, Release and Controversy

Helen Saxton

An imprint of
Pen & Sword Books Ltd
Yorkshire - Philadelphia

First published in Great Britain in 2023 by
Pen & Sword True Crime
An imprint of
Pen & Sword Books Ltd
Yorkshire - Philadelphia

Copyright © Helen Saxton, 2023

ISBN 978 1 39906 833 8

The right of Helen Saxton to be identified as the Author of this work has been asserted by him in accordance with the Copyright, Designs and Patents Act 1988.

A CIP catalogue record for this book is available from the British Library.

All rights reserved. No part of this book may be reproduced or transmitted in any form or by any means, electronic or mechanical, including photocopying, recording or by any information storage and retrieval system, without permission from the Publisher in writing.

Typeset in INDIA by IMPEC eSolutions
Printed and bound in England by CPI (UK) Ltd.

Pen & Sword Books Ltd incorporates the Imprints of Pen & Sword Archaeology, Atlas, Aviation, Battleground, Discovery, Family History, History, Maritime, Military, Naval, Politics, Railways, Select, Transport, True Crime, Fiction, Frontline Books, Leo Cooper, Praetorian Press, Seaforth Publishing, Wharncliffe and White Owl.

For a complete list of Pen & Sword titles please contact

PEN & SWORD BOOKS LIMITED
47 Church Street, Barnsley, South Yorkshire, S70 2AS, England
E-mail: enquiries@pen-and-sword.co.uk
Website: www.pen-and-sword.co.uk

or

PEN AND SWORD BOOKS
1950 Lawrence Rd, Havertown, PA 19083, USA
E-mail: uspen-and-sword@casematepublishers.com
Website: www.penandswordbooks.com

Contents

INTRODUCTION	1
Her name is Meredith	2
You are completely wrong. The evidence is clear.	5
MURDER	8
Convergence	9
Hallowtide	26
Discovery	32
It Begins	43
Suspicion	52
One Black Man for Another	68
Heading for Trial	76
TRIAL	83
George Clooney's wife	84
The First Round	98
Probable Identity	106
Reasonable Doubt	121
BEYOND	**129**
Arguing with Strangers on the Internet	130
More Questions than Answers	153
Campaign of Confusion	169

STORYTELLING	**177**
Ménage à trois	178
Innocent Bystander	182
Lone Predator	184
AMANDA	**189**
Does my name belong to me?	190
REFERENCES	**197**
Publications	198
Websites	199
Documentaries and Films	201
Podcasts	202
Online Articles	203
Endnotes	207

INTRODUCTION

Her name is Meredith

It may come as a surprise that while researching this case one of the most shocking things to emerge was not contained in the court transcripts or crime scene photos, but from the attitude of a YouTuber streaming their opinion on the case to their modest number of subscribers, some fifteen years after the murder. The video is twelve minutes long. At eleven minutes in they finally mention the victim. The YouTuber's words? 'I think her name was Meredith.'[1]

One of the online forum users who kindly agreed for our chats to be referenced in this book consistently talked about a victim named Miranda. Even after being corrected, he referred to her as Miranda again a few minutes later. His explanation? 'Meredith doesn't exist here. If you said "Meredith Kercher" people would have no clue what you are talking about at all.'[2] Now, this cannot be entirely true; he is based in the United States and one man cannot speak for a nation of 330 million, but there is a certain, depressing ring of truth to his claim. This is not the first and will not be the last case where the victim's story pales into the background in the face of a media circus surrounding the suspects, investigation and trial.

Tragically, Meredith Kercher was only alive for a very brief fragment of the story that would unfold in the days, weeks, months and years following her murder. The length of time from her arrival in Perugia to the moment her body was discovered spans a matter of weeks; in fact, she was alive for less than seventy days in Italy. And yet the investigation and subsequent trials continued in an official capacity for over seven years and the story which eventually came to light and continues to be told to this day overshadowed her memory with a kind of morbid inevitability. The circus of events which were set into motion following her senseless and brutal murder were, thankfully, not Meredith's story. Hers should have been one of promise fulfilment, a year's study in Italy followed perhaps by a successful career in journalism, and then, who knows? But tragically, this ending was cut short.

Meredith's story is one set among a loving family, a cocoon of great friends and a promising academic future. She entered the world on 28 December 1985, born to parents John and Arline in Southwark, London. She had two older brothers, Lyle and John, and was very close to her only sister Stephanie who was three years older than her. Following a school trip to Italy she had fallen in love with the country, so years later, while studying European Politics and Italian at Leeds University, she was delighted to get the chance to study in Italy for a year during her degree. From a choice of Rome, Milan and Perugia she chose the latter as, her father explains, she felt it would provide her with much more opportunity to interact with people, given its smaller size. This seems typical of the confident, outgoing and genuine Meredith he describes.

Despite her parents' separation in 1997 Meredith remained extremely close to both her mum and dad; she would speak to John daily, especially while abroad, and it was one of the reasons why she kept both an Italian and a British phone while in Perugia, for ease of communication, especially given that her mother Arline was suffering with health problems. Sadly, her parents both died in 2020, within four months of each other, but her siblings have continued to champion their sister's memory and are still searching for answers; their true justice.

It is impossible to sum up a person one has never met in a matter of paragraphs, and it would be foolish to try. However, Meredith, known affectionately as Mez, loved fashion and shopping for clothes, watching *Friends*, musical theatre, karate, chocolate, and travelling. She was always late, took ballet lessons, would dance around the house with her sister, was sensitive and kind and had a beautiful singing voice. She loved cooking, was intelligent, diligent, and enjoyed nights out with her friends. She was popular, happy and bright, with her infectious personality affecting everyone around her. Hers was a life which was full of laughter and should rise above the following, controversial story, and never be forgotten.

You are completely wrong.
The evidence is clear.

It is an unnerving fact that no one, apart from the person or persons in the room at the moment when Meredith Kercher was murdered *knows* the truth of what happened. The rest can postulate, examine, discuss and prove theories using DNA, circumstantial evidence, eyewitness testimony, or even full confessions. They can be utterly convinced one way or another, but surely, they can never actually *know*. They were not there. Rudy Guede, Amanda Knox, Raffaele Sollecito. They, and only they, *know* if they are guilty or innocent.

Of course, some cases are far clearer cut than others; Ted Bundy maintained his innocence until just before his death but there is very little argument, if any, that he was guilty of the horrific crimes he was condemned for. Jeffrey Dahmer was positively forthcoming in his detailed confessions following his arrest, which were backed up by substantial physical evidence and even survivor's testimony. But still, thankfully, we were not there. And so, we cannot say with certainty that we *know* what happened.

In the case of Meredith Kercher's murder, a fair amount of people seem to think they do, in fact, *know* what happened that night. Some *know* that Amanda and Raffaele were involved, some *know* that Rudy acted alone. By this very virtue they cannot all be correct. But they *know* they are right. There will of course be thousands of people who have an idea, a feeling, or are simply interested in the case, but those who shout the loudest are certainly very sure of their knowledge.

Unfortunately, it's easy to see why the murder of Meredith Kercher and the investigation that followed became so controversial, and so divisive. For every piece of DNA evidence suggesting guilt, there is a theory to disprove it. For every apparently innocent behaviour, there is suggestion of a sinister ulterior motive. In theory anything can be proven, depending on which way the evidence is interpreted; add into the mix a highly publicised case where the victim is a young English woman studying in Italy, with a cast of potential suspects including: a young Italian and American couple in the first week of an intense relationship, with a cloud of sex and drugs hanging over them, and an immigrant drifter stoking the fires, it's little wonder it gained such interest at the time, and that people still continue to argue about the outcome to this day.

Confirmation bias is an almost unavoidable issue in crime investigations. It's described as 'the tendency to search for, interpret, favour, and recall information in a way that confirms or supports one's prior beliefs or values',[1] and is surely a major factor in explaining why this case still causes such controversy after so many years. Believing one version of events and dismissing others which don't back up a particular theory is a key theme running throughout discussions about this case.

However, perhaps one of the main reasons for its continued interest among the true crime community is the sheer number of different outcomes at the various trials, leaving some people with a feeling that there is unfinished business to resolve. Rudy Guede was found guilty of the murder but was released from prison after serving just thirteen years. Amanda and Raffaele were convicted, had their convictions overturned, were convicted again and then finally acquitted in 2015. However, a cloud still hangs over the process, with upheld slander convictions and a clause in the final verdict still leaving some uncertain. There is, for some, the feeling that none of the suspects has ever quite been found guilty, and yet none of them have ever quite been exonerated either.

But why '*Amanda Knox*'? Why not Rudy Guede, or Raffaele Sollecito? The following chapters not only pull together a timeline of events leading up to and following the murder, but also take a deeper look at the particular pieces of evidence which cause the most controversy and crucially, examine why Amanda Knox remains this central character in this story. Although much of this stems from the media interest at the time, a look at the numerous documentaries, films, podcasts and even YouTube analyses of the case which have sprung up over the years gives some insight into why the spotlight has continued, in no small part also due to Amanda's social media presence since her release.

It seems a simple idea, to piece together a timeline of events leading up to and following the tragic murder of a British student studying abroad. And yet, inevitably, the real truth is illusory. Original court transcripts rely on interpretation; who is to say if the interpreter is biased one way or another, or the reader misinterprets the meaning of a word translated from Italian to English? Ten different books written about the case have been used as source material – in part to create a full picture, and in part to showcase just how diversely this story is told, depending on the personal views of the author. Reading one after the other, the strings which come together to form the overall story start to become tangled and out of focus. The source content differs in so many ways, with even simple facts which have no bearing on the outcome of the case slipping and sliding from book to book, making claims of a definitive revealing of the truth seem elusive, and absurd.

You may know nothing about this case. You may have heard about sex games gone wrong, cartwheels in police stations, drugs and salacious nicknames. You may think you know what happened. But what follows has been pieced together from all sides of the story, and ultimately, leaves you, the reader, to make up your own mind about what happened on that fateful night in Perugia in 2007.

MURDER

Convergence

Perugia. An Italian town, capital of the Umbrian region in whose captivating hills it is neatly nestled. Known also as the City of Chocolate, it's home to some of the most famous and delicious pralines and truffles in the world and annually hosts a ten-day festival named Eurochocolate which is, by all accounts, a chocolate lover's dream. Perugia is also, coincidentally, twinned with Seattle, Washington, hometown of Amanda Knox.

Perugia boasts two universities, the *Universita degli Studi di Perugia* (University of Perugia) which is mainly attended by native Italians, and the *Universita per Stranieri di Perugia* (University for Foreigners, sometimes known as the *Stranieri*) which, as its name suggests, caters more for overseas exchange students from around the world. Consequently, of the approximately 160,000 residents who form this relatively small town, a high proportion is made up of students, or *stranieri*.

Every city, town and village across the globe hides within it an objectionably less desirable area and Perugia is no different; its inviting, historic cobblestoned elegance rubs alongside its darker side within which thrives, among other things, an apparently brazen drugs scene. One documentary about this case described Perugia in terms of 'Dante by day, Inferno by night',[1] with the implication that when the students emerge after dark and inhabit the packed bars nestled into medieval buildings, the debauchery begins. In reality though, Perugia is a student town like many, many others and understandably a mix of its beauty and party atmosphere attracts students from all over the world.

And this is exactly where, in late August 2007, 21-year-old Meredith Kercher's anticipated year of study abroad began. Despite researching extensively while still at home in England she'd been unable to find any suitable accommodation before arriving in Italy, so having booked herself into a hotel on arrival she was soon looking for somewhere more permanent to stay. In daily contact with her family, she kept them up to date with her Italian journey and settled in seamlessly despite feeling understandably lonely in her single hotel room.

She scoured the noticeboards at the *Stranieri* for three days before coming across an advert placed by Filomena Romanelli and Laura Mezzetti, two Italian women in their late twenties who were advertising a room to rent in their cottage. Laura and Filomena gladly showed Meredith around the cottage, and once she had checked in with her dad as to whether or not the required deposit seemed appropriate, she was warmly welcomed by them when she moved in the following day.

The cottage at No. 7, Via della Pergola, would later become the centre of a murder investigation but back when Meredith first set eyes on it, it was simply a traditional villa in the middle of a town, a desirable place to stay and soak up the Umbrian atmosphere just a few minutes' walk from the university. The best of both worlds: close to the bustling centre in one direction, and delivering incredible views over the valley beyond in another. The cottage was divided into two flats with four bedrooms on the top floor occupied by Filomena, Laura, and soon to be Meredith and Amanda, and with four male students living in the semi-basement below. These students, Giacomo Silenzi, Stefano Bonassi, Marco Marzan and Riccardo Luciani, were never suspected of any involvement in Meredith's murder but would inevitably be drawn into the drama that would unfold.

So, for a brief period, Meredith embraced the Perugian culture without having ever met her future flatmate, Amanda Knox.

Universally described as caring and friendly with a great sense of humour, it's no wonder that Meredith made friends within days of arriving in Italy; friends who, despite having only known her for a few weeks by the time of her murder, clearly cherished her friendship and genuinely enjoyed her company, and not just because they were initially drawn together due to their shared nationality. According to her father, the first friend she made was Amy Frost, who had also been studying at Leeds University. Although they had not met in person, Meredith had made contact with Amy via email, along with other Leeds students Robyn Butterworth and Natalie Hayward, before leaving for Italy.

Once in Perugia Meredith met up with Amy, along with another British student, Helen Power, who had already become friends with the former. Robyn and Amy had also already met; they had previously arranged to organise accommodation together and were sharing a flat. Another student, Sophie Purton – who would turn out to be the last of Meredith's friends to see her alive – also met Meredith through Amy. They fell into a comfortable social routine familiar with many students, going out for pizza, cooking together at home, watching movies or drinking and dancing, particularly at one of their favourite hangouts, the Merlin bar in Via del Forno. Here they met another connection to their hometown – the owner Pasquale Alessi (known as Pisco) had previously studied engineering at Leeds University.

The girls weren't in Perugia just to socialise of course. They had come to Italy to study. Meredith threw herself into her work, spending each morning settling into her intensive Italian course at the university and dedicating the afternoons to improving her Italian. It seemed that everything was going perfectly to plan; she told her new friend Pisco how beautiful she found Perugia, confident that she had made the right decision to study there.

Meanwhile, almost 1,000 miles away, an American student, Amanda Knox, was visiting relatives in Hamburg, Germany, with her younger sister, Deanna, having previously made the journey to Perugia to bag the smaller of the two rooms on offer in No. 7, Via della Pergola. While in Hamburg she received an email from Laura and Filomena, letting her know that the other room had been taken by a British exchange student and, according to Amanda, urging her to get back to Perugia as soon as possible to 'get the party started'.[2]

Amanda's choice to study in Perugia seemed naturally to follow on from her education in Seattle, where she attended the University of Washington studying Italian, German and creative writing. As someone who had always enjoyed learning languages, studying Japanese among others, she was drawn to spending her junior year at university studying abroad and settled on Italian as her language of choice. According to her, she chose Perugia so that she could immerse herself in Italian culture, rather than become one of a hundred other American students if she chose to go somewhere more mainstream, like Rome for example. She was aiming for an intense course run by the language-focused *Stranieri* with the plan that by the end of the nine-month course she would be fluent in Italian and ready to move on to the next stage.

Amanda Knox was born on 9 July 1987 in Seattle, Washington, to parents Curt and Edda, who divorced when Amanda was one. At the time of the separation her mother was already pregnant with Amanda's younger sister Deanna and, by most accounts, while the couple made every effort to make the split easier on the girls, Edda and Curt themselves remained somewhat distant on a personal level. Curt moved two blocks away, creating a setup whereby Amanda and Deanna essentially had two homes to go to, although Edda recalls this period of time in a way which will resonate with many families following divorce; one where Curt got to enjoy everything fun about parenthood, while she shouldered the majority of the mundane elements like childcare and discipline.

Edda was born in Germany and had moved to Seattle when she was fairly young; a few years after her divorce she met and married Chris Mellas. Curt was by then already living with his second wife, Cassandra, with whom he had two children, Amanda's half-sisters Ashley and Delaney. According to Amanda, although she was made to feel less welcome at her father's house once the girls were born and their relationship became more distant during her teenage years, both of her biological parents continued to remain incredibly supportive of her.

Amanda's journey to Perugia was, by all accounts, fairly eventful and understandably she relays it from perhaps a naïve and romantic point of view in her memoirs. However, even at this point in the narrative, later interpretations looking back on her alleged behaviour on that journey are already incredibly diverse.

According to Amanda's memoirs, Deanna accompanied her on the first visit with the aim of finding accommodation, taking a train from Milan to Florence where they would stop over for one night before continuing by train to Perugia the following day. Amanda had an encounter with a man on that first train; casual flirting led to sharing a joint, followed by her 'first bona fide one-night stand',[3] according to her blog at the time. This account later changed in her memoirs as she explains that they 'didn't have a condom so we didn't actually have intercourse'.[4] The following day she and Deanna arrived in Perugia by train and decided to walk from the station to the town but severely misjudged the distance. They eventually accepted a lift from a 40-something man who half-heartedly tried to flirt with them before dropping them off at their hotel.

Conversely, some accounts spin this journey in a very different way, not by changing the facts but by the way in which language is used to describe them. Amanda is, for example, 'hit on by a pervy Italian motorist twice her age',[5] and her encounter on the train is often described with an air of negative judgement about her sex life. This judgement would, of course, become much more intense in November.

Back on that first day in Perugia though, she and Deanna came across Laura pinning up the advert for the spare rooms to rent in No. 7, Via della Pergola. Wasting no time, they viewed the cottage which Amanda described as 'fit for a fairy tale',[6] following which she immediately agreed to take one of the rooms. She and her sister then left for Hamburg to stay with their Aunt Dolly; Deanna would then head back to Seattle, with Amanda returning to Perugia in time to start her course in October.

Even this early in the narrative, the order in which Amanda and Meredith viewed and chose their rooms can be confusing. Both Amanda, and Meredith's father John Kercher, explain that Amanda was the first of the two girls to visit the cottage. She had the pick of the two rooms available and despite its size, Amanda chose the smaller room as she thought it was cosy and exactly what she was looking for. Meredith was shown the remaining room when she arrived in late August and was told by Laura and Filomena that an American girl had already taken the other room and was due to move in a month or so later. Other accounts describe Amanda as having no choice but to take the smallest remaining room and that, a couple of weeks after Meredith moved in, Laura and Filomena told her that an American girl would be taking the small room. Ultimately the order of events has no impact at all on the outcome of the case, but the differing accounts are indicative of how difficult, if even possible, it can be to keep track of its truth.

Either way, Amanda returned to Perugia and moved into the cottage on 20 September 2007. The lives of these two students converged for the first time, both now finding their feet in a foreign country and sharing the cottage which, in just a matter of weeks, would become the scene of an horrific murder. On the top floor, Meredith and Amanda's rooms were next door to each other, with a shared bathroom in the hallway just outside Meredith's room. Double doors opposite the girls' doors led to a small terrace overlooking the valley. Filomena's room was situated next to Amanda's and led into the living and kitchen area, as did Laura's from the opposite side of the room. Next to Laura's room was the bigger bathroom, shared by her and Filomena.

Accounts of the atmosphere in the cottage during the matter of weeks between the girls moving in and the night of Meredith's murder differ extremely depending on the source, and will ultimately paint either a benign picture of two women sharing a cottage, companionable but not the best of friends, or conversely, a hotbed of tension building up between two mis-matched young women living in close proximity.

It is inevitable that the atmosphere surrounding this period of time is contentious. Amanda was ultimately accused of killing Meredith, with one of the proposed motives being that she became fed up with her prudish ways and wanted to teach her a lesson. For this narrative to ring true, Amanda and Meredith must be shown to have harboured a considerable amount of animosity. Amanda's accounts play down any arguments as unconfrontational – in direct contradiction to those who think she may be guilty, and who tell quite a different story.

Meredith had already made numerous friends by the time Amanda arrived and everyone seems to agree that initially they got on fairly well; Meredith was a year-and-a-half older than Amanda and took her under her wing, showing her around Perugia and introducing her to her friends, inviting her on nights out. After a few days though, she and her friends started to think of Amanda's behaviour as slightly odd; commenting that 'the things she does, they're a bit weird'.[7] In the first documentary made about the case, which aired in 2008 before the initial trial verdict, the narrator describes the fact that the girls had 'separate rooms and separate friends',[8] and emphasises the tensions between them, stating very clearly that Meredith's friends did not like Amanda. The main points of contention seemed to be her lack of hygiene and helping to keep the house clean, and that she would regularly bring men back to the house, which made Meredith nervous. By contrast, the Netflix documentary in which Amanda participated, aired in 2016 after the final verdict had been announced, plays down the tensions and essentially describes the usual niggles to be expected when sharing accommodation with virtual strangers.

The opinions of Meredith's friends about Amanda's behaviour would become stronger after the murder, but for now, and no matter what their level of personal differences, by all accounts Meredith and Amanda were intelligent and keen students, and had both fallen in love with Perugia, and were happily settled by mid-October.

With the benefit of hindsight, even the most apparently inconsequential events now seem to be converging towards the night of the murder on 1 November. One such run-of-the-mill occurrence was that Amanda decided she needed to earn some money to supplement her savings and relieve a certain amount of boredom, having been disappointed in, and feeling unchallenged by, the work she was set by the university. She wanted a job. Nobody could have foretold the impact this decision would have on the forthcoming murder investigation, but does the way in which she got this job really impact on her perceived guilt or innocence? And if not, why are there varying versions of how Amanda came to work at Le Chic?

It's undisputed that Amanda started working at the pub run by a local immigrant from Zaire, Diya 'Patrick' Lumumba, who had been living in Italy for seventeen years. It's how she arrived there, her attitude to the job and her relationship with Patrick that differs. Amanda's account is that in early October she chatted with Laura about looking for work, who then introduced her to a friend of hers named Juve. His boss, Patrick, was just getting his new pub Le Chic off the ground and, following an informal interview that was little more than a casual chat, Juve suggested that she hand flyers out at the *Stranieri*, then work in the bar from 9.00pm to 1.00am. Her duties were basically to bring the customers in, and make sure they had a good time, which she says she struggled with slightly – partly due to the language barrier and needing Juve to translate Patrick's instructions, and partly because she said the job made her feel 'used and unsure'[9] of herself.

Other accounts tell a very different tale and paint Amanda as an inadequate employee, ranging from simply being inept at the job to openly flirting with every male in sight. Some say that Amanda first attempted to get a job at the Bear's Lair pub, run by an English woman called Lucy Rigby. As she had just recently filled a vacancy, Lucy directed Amanda to her friend Patrick's new bar, Le Chic. Amanda went for a drink at the pub, accompanied by Meredith, who outshone her immediately, impressing Patrick with her cocktail-making skills and creating an amazing Mojito with Polish vodka. Patrick was so impressed that he offered her a job, but as she would be too busy with her studies to take it on, he grudgingly hired Amanda to work from 8.00pm to 3.00am after she asked for work.

As will become apparent throughout the investigation, this account is key in sowing the seeds of a less than happy employer/employee relationship between Patrick and Amanda. It becomes even more obvious following a scene from the 2011 made for TV film *Amanda Knox, Murder on Trial in Italy*, which was aired after their first conviction but before their first appeal. Although the whole film presents a sanitised, romanticised version of events which portrays Amanda as essentially innocent, this is the one scene in which there is a nod to the implied animosity between the two girls. When Patrick praises Meredith's cocktail-making skills and suggests he would like to employ her, Amanda appears less than thrilled, to say the least.

Patrick would become a key male player in this case, but in the meantime two more men were weaving their way into the narrative;

firstly, in the shape of a 21-year-old by the name of Rudy Guede. A native of Ivory Coast who moved to Italy at the age of 5, Rudy had a troubled relationship with his father, eventually resulting in him being fostered by a rich and well-respected couple called the Caporalis. Through school he formed a bond with a teacher, Ivana Tiberi, who would later be described as a surrogate mother figure and a hugely positive influence in his life. Rudy's background becomes more significant later in the narrative, but for now, and by all accounts, Rudy was a fully integrated Italian and spoke the language perfectly, even with a Perugian accent. Although he would deny any criminal activity in his background, at the very least it is clear that Rudy did not have a stable lifestyle or job, and by the time he was 19 in the spring of 2007, he was living with an aunt in Lecco, a small town near Milan some 300 miles away from Perugia.

Varying accounts have him working as a waiter in Pavia during this time, after which he headed back to Perugia. He initially stayed with Ivana, following which the Caporalis found him a job as a gardener. Rudy continually found it difficult to hold down a job and this time was no different; he apparently then spent the rest of 2007 until his arrest in November living off his savings, playing basketball in the Piazza Grimana and hanging out with various friends he had made in Perugia. He is consistently portrayed as a drifter, although he seemed to make friends easily and moved in Perugia's student circles. He lived in a tiny flat and many accounts say that he had a habit of taking on different personas, pretending to be someone he was not; sometimes a South African, sometimes an American who went by the name of Kevin. He revelled in the intriguing and mysterious nickname he had picked up, The Baron.

So how did his path cross with Amanda and Meredith's? If he tended to hang out with students then it's not too much of a leap to imagine that they would meet, but again, accounts are conflicted and this time, it's easy to see why. If Amanda is guilty of killing Meredith with Rudy as a willing accomplice, as the first trial suggested and succeeded in proving, then their relationship needs to have been established in order to make sense of it. If she's innocent, the narrative must be that she and Meredith barely knew him.

According to Amanda, in mid-October, sometime after she had started working at Le Chic, she was walking home after a quiet night when the bar had closed early. She bumped into Giacomo and Marco, two of the residents in the downstairs flat, and accepted a beer from the former, who had fairly recently started a casual relationship with Meredith. After the meeting Amanda went off to find Meredith and the two of them met up with the boys again shortly afterwards, at which point they introduced her to their friend Rudy, with whom they often played basketball. They all walked back to the cottage together and Meredith and Amanda dropped their things upstairs before joining the boys downstairs for a joint. Tired, Amanda soon went to bed leaving Meredith with them in the downstairs flat. In her memoirs, she doesn't ever mention meeting Rudy again. It was a fleeting introduction, and she had no cause to think of him after that.

At least two other accounts, including one directly from Rudy, have them meeting at least one more time, apparently when Rudy visited Le Chic and encountered her there. One account claims that 'Amanda also remembered he'd tried to chat her up in one of the bars',[10] and, according to Rudy's court testimony, having been being handed a leaflet he decided to try out the new bar, Le Chic. Amanda was working, they chatted about Seattle as he had a friend who had attended the University of Washington, but the conversation ended there.

It seems that most people agree that, even if Amanda wasn't present, Rudy did visit the boys' flat at least once more, arriving uninvited to watch the Grand Prix with them on 21 October. On this occasion it may be that Laura came downstairs and met Rudy for the first time, although Filomena did not. Perhaps understandably, none of the boys from the flat downstairs appear to take any responsibility for being the one who introduced Rudy into the house. He was just a drifter who appeared at parties; Stefano told the police that he had no idea if it was Amanda, Meredith, Laura, Filomena, or one of the other boys who had first brought him to the house. However, in an ominous foreshadowing of what was to come, the boys say that on the night that Amanda did meet Rudy, he had got drunk, gone to the toilet, and fallen asleep while still sitting on it. Later, he woke up and went to crash on their sofa, leaving the toilet unflushed.

Unsolicited opinions on Amanda's sex life seem to be key, if not to the entire investigation (although they certainly played a major part in the prosecution establishing a motive), then certainly to the press coverage of the case. Even before the second main male character appeared in Amanda's life and story, she would meet a few other men in Perugia. Did this have anything to do with the murder? On the face of it, no; but to many it supports the narrative of simmering tensions between Meredith and Amanda. In her book, she describes a friend, Spyros, a Greek man who ran an internet café she frequented. At no point does she mention a sexual relationship with him, but other accounts describe Meredith and her friends disliking the fact that he frequented the cottage; they found him strange and had dubbed him 'Internet Man'.[11]

Amanda also describes her first proper one-night stand since arriving in Perugia, a slightly awkward affair with a barista whom she calls Mirko. She fancied him, they flirted, they ended up at his place, simple. On another occasion she, Meredith, Giacomo and some of the boys' friends, hung out at a local club, drank a fair amount, and Amanda ended up sleeping with one of the friends, Bobby, in her bedroom at the cottage that night. It was on the same night that Meredith first slept with Giacomo in his apartment downstairs.

Her accounts of these relationships, and the way in which she spoke about them to her flatmates, appears perfectly normal for a group of twenty-something girls. It was all very open; they gave each other advice and Laura even insisted that they should not overthink it and just go out and have fun. Amanda's night with Mirko is portrayed as a kind of coming-of-age story, she felt rather flat the following day and confided in Meredith and the others about her feelings. They were all girlfriends together, sympathetic, cool and supportive. Her night with Bobby was, she says, the first time she had brought anyone back to stay with her in a sexual context and although the following morning was a bit awkward, it was no big deal. The implication was that everyone had enjoyed a bit of a wild night, but it was not an experience that she nor anyone else was planning to repeat.

Amanda had developed a cold sore since arriving in Italy, perhaps due to her fooling around with the guy back on her journey with Deanna on the train. At the club, she says that Bobby pointed out her cold sore, sympathetically encouraging her not to worry or be self-conscious about it. Curiously, a separate account of the night names the man as Daniel De Luna, who rudely drew attention to the embarrassing sore, opining that she must really love sex if she's got herpes. The fact that, in this account, she still chose to spend the night with him despite his clear rudeness and ignorance puts an altogether different spin on it, with a shameless Amanda not caring who she ends up with so long as he's male. In another even more tabloid version of events, Amanda was apparently out scouring for men that night and, furious that the earlier 'Internet Man' had tried it on with Meredith, had decided to retaliate by 'picking up Giacomo's cousin'[12] and taking him home, as if he had no say in the matter. In fact, this same account says that Amanda had been looking around for male company since her arrival in Italy and had left condoms littered around the cottage as if she might need one urgently at any moment.

Whether or not the condom claim is true, Amanda had brought a vibrator with her to Italy, a joke gift from a good friend back in

Seattle. To her, it was a slightly embarrassing novelty, left casually in the shared bathroom in a see-through toiletries bag as she had no intention of actually using it, and therefore didn't feel the need to hide it. According to Meredith's friends however, Meredith found it all too much, the openness in her conversations about sex and the flaunting of a sex toy. Why couldn't she just keep it hidden somewhere discreet? Her friends were wary of what they saw as Amanda's overt sexuality, that she would sleep with men because she could, without any need for emotional connection or romance. In due course, the vibrator would be brought up in court as evidence of Amanda's promiscuity.

A Moroccan man named Hicham Khiri would come under particular suspicion later on in the investigation; he was an acquaintance of Meredith's and her friends, who met him in a club and nicknamed him Shaky because of the way he danced. According to Amanda, he offered her a ride home from Le Chic on his scooter one night, but it was not a pleasant or straightforward experience. Instead of taking her directly home he tried to persuade her to go out with him first, taking her back to his flat on the pretext of fetching something and offering her a beer. After putting her foot down and saying no, he grudgingly took her home. Again, her account of Meredith's reaction to her distress shows a normal relationship between two flatmates; she was furious about Shaky's behaviour and Meredith was duly sympathetic, explaining that he'd pulled a similar trick with Sophie previously and that none of the girls particularly liked him; on one occasion, he'd even taken his trousers down in front of Meredith at a club, much to their slightly drunken horror.

Meredith's relationship with Giacomo, while not completely serious, seemed to be developing into something more than just a one-off. Her friends tell the story of when she had first confided in Amanda that she really liked him. Amanda announced that she, too, fancied him, but graciously said she would allow Meredith to have him. Not surprisingly, Amanda does not mention this story in her memoirs, but it is corroborated by Meredith's friends.

The second male figure waiting in the wings to enter Amanda's story, who one author describes as 'her fourth conquest',[13] had just taken his last undergraduate exam for his bachelor's degree in computer science at the *Universita degli Studi di Perugia* on 25 October 2007 when a chance encounter led to his meeting Amanda Knox at an altogether more civilised event than the way in which she had met Rudy Guede.

Raffaele Sollecito was born on 26 March 1984 in Giovinazzo, a small town near Bari in southern Italy. He was by all accounts a coddled child, particularly by his mother, although he also had a very close relationship with his father, Francesco. His parents divorced when he was 8 years old, something he says was devastating for his mother, while his father started a new life fairly soon afterwards with a lady called Mara, whom he would later marry. Raffaele had a sister, Vanessa, who was six years older than him and who would go on to join the *Carabinieri*, the Italian police force.

An apparently shy child, Raffaele selected Perugia as his university of choice in part to distance himself from his parents' overbearing relationship (there is a distance of around 350 miles between the two towns). His mother died in 2005, while he was in Perugia and although her cause of death was given as a heart attack, Raffaele strenuously denies rumours that she had committed suicide. Having previously lived in halls of residence, by 2006 Raffaele had moved into the studio apartment in Corso Garibaldi, where he was living when he met Amanda. His accommodation, with maid service, was expensive, but the rent seems to have been covered by his wealthy father. He owned an Audi, and certainly did not want for anything in the material sense.

On 25 October, having just completed a final assignment for his course, Raffaele headed out with a friend to a Quintetto Bottesini concert at the *Universita per Stranieri di Perugia's* Great Hall. Amanda and Meredith were also in attendance, and after an introduction of Astor Piazzolla's Grand Tango, the crowd dispersed into an interval during which Meredith left the concert to meet friends for dinner, leaving a spare seat for Raffaele to slip into, following some flirty eye contact between himself and Amanda during the previous recital.

It's clear from both Amanda and Raffaele's romanticised accounts of this meeting that they are keen to portray themselves as young, innocent lovers. Raffaele reminisces about the moment he fell in love with Amanda as when he was hit by 'un colpo di fulmine', or lightning bolt under a 'star-filled Perugian sky'. When they kissed for the first time 'it was intense and beautiful and seemed to last forever'.[14] Amanda recalls inviting Raffaele to come and meet her at work at Le Chic that night, spending the rest of the evening in a state of nervous anticipation, feeling her stomach do a 'nervous flip'[15] when he eventually arrived with some friends. He walked her back to his place, and they had sex. After that, they were inseparable. By the time Meredith was murdered, Amanda and Raffaele had known each other for a week, and had spent the majority of that time in each other's company, fooling around and smoking pot.

Some will list Raffaele as just another man in a long line of conquests for Amanda, and from the very moment they met, retrospectively all eyes would be studying the relationship with a myriad of different interpretations made about their togetherness. Where they describe a blindly romantic union, others saw it differently; Laura and Filomena seemed unnerved by how clingy they were, with tales of Raffaele following Amanda around the apartment like a small puppy, constantly hugging her and covering her with kisses. Amanda stayed most nights at the 23-year-old's house and went back to her cottage every day for clean clothes and to shower; although his apartment was arguably better equipped, she preferred to shower at home; her clothes and belongings were there, and Raffaele's bathroom was too cramped.

By now, Meredith's friends say that the relationship had started to cool between the two girls. All accounts seem to agree that Amanda wasn't quite pulling her weight with the cleaning, and Meredith had been embarrassed to have to point out to her that she was often leaving the toilet unflushed and dirty. All accounts agree that this was by no means an argument, but it was certainly an example of issues bubbling under the surface coming to a head; the type of incident which is generally common in shared accommodation. This particular bugbear would turn out to be much more significant later on.

Meredith and her friends all continued to find Amanda a little weird, grating, even embarrassing. On one night out she allegedly poured a drink over a stranger's head, she insisted on speaking Italian loudly all the time, with her mistakes grating on the others. She was an extrovert, and it irritated them. Their impression of her was that of an attention seeker, particularly vying for male attention if she felt it was wandering elsewhere. She had at one point told Meredith that she preferred to socialise with Italians in order to help with the language, essentially snubbing her and her British friends. So, after a few weeks the wider social group had settled in to a full but not excessive social life with some niggles and tensions starting to show. Amanda herself seemed, if anything, oblivious to how her behaviour affected the others; where she described herself as quirky, the others might counter with their own view – she was irritating.

Hallowtide

Halloween doesn't enjoy the same cultural significance in Italy as it does in the United States. Italians focus more on All Saint's Day which falls on 1 November and is dedicated to remembering those who are no longer living. However, with a town full of foreign students to cater for there were parties aplenty in Perugia on 31 October 2007; according to Amanda it is 'the number one money-making night of the year'[1] in the town. Raffaele explains that Halloween is a huge deal for the foreign students but 'not a big deal to us Italians'.[2]

The series of events which took place on Halloween and All Saint's Day in Perugia in 2007 were to culminate in an horrendous murder in No. 7, Via della Pergola. But which of them were significant, and which were simply the actions of a group of people enjoying the Halloween celebrations? Raffaele was not particularly interested in partying, Meredith and her friends went all out with their costumes, and Amanda bar-hopped for a while before heading home fairly early compared to the other girls.

Amanda and Meredith's separate Halloween plans could be viewed as indicative of their failing relationship, depending on something as simple as the interpretation of a text exchange between the two of them that night. By Amanda's own account she sent Meredith a quick message on Halloween:

> A: 'what are you doing tonight? Want to meet up? Got a costume?'
> M: 'yes, I have one, but I have to go to a friend's house for dinner. What are your plans? X'[3]

This seems fairly innocuous, until other accounts change up the order of the text. One suggests that Amanda first asked what Meredith was up to, which she replied to with the above message about going to a friend's for dinner. This version has Amanda following up with her message about costumes and meeting up, followed in quick succession by another suggesting 'I'm going to Le Chic and after who knows? Maybe we'll meet up? Call me',[4] to which Meredith never responded. This exchange portrays Amanda as much more desperate, persisting for an answer which never came, giving more weight to the idea that it was a deliberate snub. In a way Raffaele confirms this, saying that Meredith's friends did not like Amanda, and that Meredith never responded to Amanda's suggestion to meet. If the smouldering tensions between Meredith and Amanda are to be believed, this may well have inflamed more animosity.

Whether or not this animosity was present, they did not spend Halloween together. Meredith, Sophie, Robyn, Natalie and two other friends met at Amy's house where they ate dinner before putting their costumes together and heading out to their favourite haunt, The Merlin pub. When this closed at around 2.00am they moved on to the Domus nightclub, where Meredith sat at a table chatting to friends. She suggested heading home at around 3.30am and they ended up parting ways at about 4.00am, arranging to meet again at Amy's later on that day to chill out with a film and dinner after their late night.

Some of the more sensationalised accounts describe that Meredith 'party-hopped'[5] until 6.30am, with Amanda partying elsewhere until around 5.00am. Amanda herself says that she didn't think much of the party scene and was nostalgic for Seattle; she had a couple of drinks at Le Chic and then walked home with Raffaele at around 1.45am. Raffaele confirms that Amanda was out with Spyros, possibly at The Merlin, but that she didn't cross paths with Meredith who had already headed off to the Domus by the time Amanda arrived.

The question of whether or not Amanda and Meredith met up that night is not nearly so significant as ascertaining whether or not Meredith and Rudy's paths crossed. Some accounts say that they met at the Domus nightclub that night and even go so far as to say that she danced with him. Rudy himself claims that he met up with Meredith at 'some kid's house' where he asked her if she wanted to 'suck up my blood because you lost the cup?',[6] in reference to when he claims to have first met her – watching England lose to South Africa in the Rugby World Cup final during a phase when he was pretending to be a South African. Rudy's motivation for asserting that they not only met, but kissed, would become significant in his defence later on, of course. During a rare interview he gave on Italian television in 2016, Rudy portrays himself as quite the ladies' man, and is adamant that both Meredith and Amanda were attracted to him, but it was Meredith with whom he shared a consensual kiss on Halloween night. Meredith's friends do not recall her meeting Rudy at a Halloween party, or at the Domus nightclub.

Despite the differing accounts, there's no doubt that Halloween was a late and probably fairly boozy night for the girls and subsequently, everyone enjoyed a relatively quiet day on 1 November. Most agree on everyone's movements, certainly as regards the earlier part of the day. Amanda headed back from Raffaele's to No. 7, Via della Pergola just before noon and chatted briefly with Filomena and her boyfriend, Marco, before Meredith appeared, having just woken up.

The group chatted, and at some point, Raffaele turned up and cooked and ate pasta with Amanda. Meredith left to go to a friend's house at around 4.00–5.00pm, after which Amanda and Raffaele headed back to his apartment for a quiet night in, with Amanda insisting that they must watch *Amelie*, a favourite film of hers which Raffaele had never seen and which she was keen to share with him. Meanwhile, Meredith spent the afternoon and evening with Sophie,

Amy and Robyn at the latter's flat, with Robyn recalling that 'the afternoon of 1 November was one of the most wonderful I have spent. We all chatted for ages, ate a meal, watched a movie, and it was all so relaxed.'[7] Tired, Meredith left her friends shortly before 9.00pm accompanied by Sophie, who walked with her back to around 500 metres of her front door. Here they parted ways for what would be the last time.

And this, of course, is where it all gets rather confusing. Or does it? If Amanda's account is to be believed, then the rest of the day and evening simply continued as planned, at least for her and Raffaele. And that account goes like this:

Not long after arriving at Raffaele's flat at around 5.50pm a friend of his, Jovanna Popovic, called by to ask him a favour. Her mother was planning on sending a suitcase via bus for Jovanna to collect, which would be arriving at the bus station at around midnight. Would Raffaele mind giving her a lift to pick it up? Raffaele agreed, and after Jovanna had left, he and Amanda settled down to watch *Amelie*, as planned. At around 8.30pm Amanda suddenly remembered that it was Thursday, and that she should be working at Le Chic that night. Hastily checking her phone, she saw that Patrick had already sent her a text telling her not to bother coming in; it was quiet in the pub and as it was a holiday, he anticipated that business would be very slow that evening. She responded with, '*Ci vediamo piu tardi bonna serata!*', which she translates as, 'See you later. Have a good evening!'[8]

Their good mood at her having been given the night off was improved even more when Jovanna reappeared at 8.45pm to say that she didn't need a lift after all. The rest of the evening was spent chilling in each other's company; the film finished at 9.15pm after which they cooked fish and ate it with salad. They washed the dishes and realised that the sink was leaking, so Amanda made plans to bring the mop from her apartment the following day to help him clear up the water. They smoked a joint or two, Amanda read *Harry Potter* to Raffaele in German. They had sex. They fell asleep and did not wake until the following morning.

This account is, of course, hotly disputed by anyone other than those who agree that Amanda and Raffaele are completely innocent of any involvement of the crime. At this stage, there was no concrete evidence emerging to suggest that Amanda and Raffaele were lying. Later, more witnesses would come forward but according to initial witnesses, some unusual activity that evening began to build up a picture of the movements surrounding No. 7, Via della Pergola.

According to some reports, a CCTV camera caught Meredith as she walked home, just after the same camera had picked up a grainy image of a 'shadowy figure' following the same route she was to take. A 'tall athletic' man was also seen passing by in the same direction.[9] At 7.41pm a camera clocked the image of a white man heading towards the girls' cottage, leaving again twenty minutes later and returning again after half an hour and heading again to the cottage. At 8.43pm the image captures a lone 'woman in a white skirt' which some suggest could have been Amanda, heading back towards the cottage.

Nara Capezzali, who lived opposite the girls' cottage, later reported that at around 11.00pm on 1 November she heard 'an agonising scream',[10] followed by what sounded like someone running on the iron staircase opposite and then a scurrying sound, 'as if someone was running along the cottage's drive of stones and dry leaves'.[11] Differing accounts place this happening at any time between 10.00pm and 11.30pm. Capezzali was known to take laxatives and later testified she had gone to sleep at around 9.00pm and the laxatives had caused her to wake up a couple of hours later, although she hadn't specifically looked at the clock.

Meanwhile, Antonella Monacchia, who lived just a few yards further up the hill, also later reported that at 11.00pm she heard the loud, agitated voices of a male and female, speaking in Italian, followed by a 'very loud scream, a woman's scream'. An Italian couple, Alessandra Formica and her boyfriend, also apparently nearly collided with a 'coloured man' running in the opposite direction near Via della Pergola at around 10.30pm.[12]

Discovery

Whatever happened on the night of 1 November, it wasn't until the following day that a sequence of seemingly unconnected events led to the discovery that something horrific had taken place in No. 7, Via della Pergola. However, the events on 2 November create arguably the most confusing and controversial chapter in this story; in part, because it relies on an account given by two people accused of murder with no witnesses to back up or disprove what they assert is the truth, and in part because of a series of discrepancies in the timeline relating to the discovery of the crime.

The structure of the Italian police force can be difficult to navigate, but essentially it consists of two main forces: the *Polizia di Stato* and the *Carabinieri*. The *Polizia* are the state or civilian police who deal with, among other things, clerical matters such as updating passports for example, as opposed to the *Carabinieri* who are the military police charged with keeping public order. However, one subsection of the *Polizia di Stato* consists of the *Squadra Mobile*, (Flying Squad) who are the emergency arm of the law, available 24/7. They may well be called out to attend the discovery of a murder, for example, although the *Carabinieri* might equally be on hand for such cases.

Both forces work together under the *Magistrato del Pubblico Ministero* (Public Prosecuting Magistrates) and a murder might be assigned on a 'first come first served' basis, depending on who is called and who turns up first. There is, if not distinct rivalry, then certainly no love lost between the *Polizia* and the *Carabinieri*. Another arm of the *Polizia di Stato* and particularly relevant to this case is the *Polizia*

Postale e Delle Comunicazioni (postal and communication police) who deal with internet and postal fraud.

On the evening of 1 November Elisabetta Lana, who lived about 400 yards from the cottage, had called the *Polizia Postale* following a phone call she had received 'announcing a bomb in one of her toilets', and she was understandably in fear of being broken into, or worse. The police arrived, scoured the house, found nothing and left. Her son, Alessandro, headed over to check that she was safe and to stay the night; the following morning at around 10.00am, he found a Motorola phone in their garden 'about six feet from the wall separating the property from the street'.[1] They assumed it belonged to one of the police officers from the previous night, and took it in to the *Polizia Postale*. Later that day, at around 11.50am, they found another phone in the garden, close to where the Motorola had been discovered: a Sony Ericsson, which happened to ring while it was in Lana's possession, with the name 'Amanda' flashing up on the screen. She also took this phone to the *Polizia Postale*, where they traced the SIM card to Filomena Romanelli, and despatched officers Michele Battistelli and Fabio Marzi to No. 7, Via della Pergola to investigate and return the phones.

The discovery of these phones might at first glance appear unimportant. The sequence of finding them is, however, crucial; not only because they ultimately proved to belong to the murder victim, but also because they triggered the arrival of police officers, albeit from the *Polizia Postale*, at the scene of the murder before the murder was discovered, rather than the state police or *Carabinieri* being called direct to investigate the discovery of a body.

While the exact timings of the discovery of the phones that morning varies from account to account it essentially has no effect on what happens next. What does matter, however, is the time that Battistelli and Marzi were despatched, and therefore exactly what time they arrived at the cottage that morning. To some, this becomes extremely relevant later on in the narrative. Most accounts agree that the officers were despatched sometime around or just after midday, but it's the time that they actually arrived at the cottage which causes most discussion and which is most crucial. Ultimately, they, and Amanda and Raffaele disagree.

Before the arrival of the *Polizia Postale* on the scene however, the narrative relies solely on Amanda's account, largely corroborated by Raffaele's account, of what happened on the morning of 2 November 2007. This account, explaining the scene which the *Polizia Postale* found themselves stumbling upon that morning, would have to be taken at face value to begin with. That account goes like this:

While the phones were being dealt with elsewhere and unbeknownst to Amanda, she meanwhile returned to the cottage to use the shower; she disliked the one at Raffaele's apartment, and besides, her clean clothes and toiletries where at her cottage. Although she doesn't specify in her memoirs what time this happened, Raffaele says that she left his house at around 9.30am to make the five to ten-minute walk back. When she arrived, she found the front door open which she thought strange, but not too alarming as its latch was ineffective and wouldn't always catch unless the door was locked with a key.

She headed to the smaller bathroom to take a shower, the one nearest her and Meredith's bedrooms, and it was here that she noticed 'two pea-size flecks'[2] of blood on the sink which she dismissed as potentially having dripped from her recently pierced ears. She took a shower, and it was only when she got out that she noticed 'a reddish-brown splotch about the size of an orange'[3] on the shower mat. She acknowledged that this may also be blood and put it down to possible menstrual issues of Meredith's.

She then headed to the bigger bathroom down the hall to borrow Laura's hair dryer. It was here that she found faeces in the toilet which 'freaked her out'[4] and it was only at this point that she began to think that perhaps there was, or had been, an intruder in the house. She grabbed the mop and made her way back to Raffaele's house to share with him what had happened and to ask if he thought it as alarming as she did.

On her way back to Raffaele's she called her mother, who told her to tell Raffaele and her flatmates, and to call her back with an update. She then called Filomena who urged her to call Meredith, which she did immediately, first trying her British phone, followed by the Italian, with no answer from either. While back at Raffaele's and in the process of explaining what had happened, she received a further call from Filomena asking what she had found at the cottage, at which point she told her that they weren't there yet. They were just planning on heading back over to the cottage now.

On arrival they investigated in more detail and discovered a broken window in Filomena's bedroom, with glass 'everywhere' and clothes 'heaped all over the bed and floor'.[5] Assuming a break-in, they checked further, only to discover that nothing appeared to have been stolen. Filomena called again, and Amanda told her about the suspected break-in.

It was only now that Amanda checked Meredith's bedroom door to discover it locked. She knocked, first quietly and then more frantically to no answer. Amanda tried to peer in from the balcony outside but could not see in, and Raffaele tried to kick the door down to no avail. Amanda says that at this point she checked the toilet in the larger bathroom again, and this time thought that the faeces had been flushed away, alarming her further.

Amanda then called to update her mother, who told her to call the police. Raffaele called his sister, a police officer. On her advice he then called 112, the emergency number for the *Carabinieri*. Amanda doesn't go into any detail about the call, simply that once he had hung up, they went to wait outside for the police to arrive. Given that Raffaele had only just placed the call, she was surprised when two officers arrived shortly afterwards, before it became apparent that they were on the scene for an entirely different reason – to return two lost phones. Shortly after this, Filomena and her friend Paolo and their respective boyfriends Marco and Luca also arrived at the cottage.

So, here the narrative is picked up and corroborated, or not, by the *Polizia Postale* and the flatmates all converging at the cottage at roughly the same time. Having established that both phones belonged to Meredith, an increasingly worried Filomena took charge and asked the police officers to break down Meredith's door. They were hesitant, they were the *Polizia Postale*, it was not within their authority to go around kicking doors down.

Taking matters into his own hands, Luca then kicked at the door repeatedly before managing to break it open. According to Amanda, almost immediately Filomena shouted out '*Un piede! Un piede!*' ('A foot! A foot!'), and although she couldn't see into Meredith's room, she heard one of the men shout out '*Sangue! Dio mio!*' ('Blood! My God!'). Battistelli finally took charge and ushered everyone out of the house. Once outside, she heard someone say the word *armadio* (armoire or closet) and *corpo* (a body), from which she imagined a scene containing 'a body inside the wardrobe with a foot sticking out'.[6]

Raffaele picks up the narrative here and says that at the moment the door was opened he was 'several people back' in the crowded corridor and that Amanda was farther back still, talking to her mother on the phone in Seattle. He also heard voices screaming about blood and 'a foot'; as this was happening, he heard Amanda explain to her mother about the foot, and then hang up. He also explains that 'one of the others mentioned seeing blood on the wall and a body laid out in front of an open closet', and that Amanda had only heard the latter part of this sentence, thus picturing Meredith in her closet.

In terms of the arrival of the rest of the police, Amanda is vague, and simply says that 'paramedics, investigators, and white-suited forensic scientists arrived in waves', and it was from one of these that Luca gained the knowledge that Meredith's throat had been 'slashed'. She felt compelled to tell one of the officers, whom she names as Monica Napoleoni, about the faeces in the toilet and the fact that it had been there one minute and gone the next. Napoleoni went to check, and on returning abruptly told her 'The faeces is still there. What are you talking about?'[7]

It's a neat explanation of the events of the day, but it's here that the first questions start to arise. The first point of contention is the order of the arrival (or non-arrival) of the police, and the order in which the phone calls were made during that period of time. Perhaps understandably, both Amanda and Raffaele's versions of the timeline are rather vague, but eagle-eyed web sleuths (and, of course, investigators at the time) have delved much more deeply into the logistics, throwing up a few issues. In a nutshell, those who believe that Amanda and Raffaele are lying about the sequence of events believe they also lied about calling the *Carabinieri*. But why?

Amanda and Raffaele assert that they called the *Carabinieri* before the *Polizia Postale* arrived. Phone records confirm that Raffaele placed the call to his sister at 12.50, then called the *Carabinieri* firstly at 12.51 followed by another call at 12.54. Battistelli's report states that they arrived at the cottage at 12.35. If this is correct, then Raffaele is lying, and must have called the *Carabinieri* after the arrival of the *Polizia Postale*. It may seem inconsequential as to when the calls were placed, but for many this is clearly a sign of guilt and supports the narrative that Amanda and Raffaele were not at the cottage innocently discovering a break-in, but were in fact in the act of cleaning up after a murder they participated in when they were surprised by the sudden and unexpected arrival of the police. Placing a call to the *Carabinieri* was their way of showing willing, to prove that they were doing their bit to help.

The defence argument centres around the claim that there is proof on CCTV from a nearby garage camera that the *Polizia Postale* in fact arrived at 12.58. They assert that the footage, albeit showing only some feet, some trouser legs and partial sightings of a car alleged to be the one driven by Battistelli that day, proves that the car did initially arrive at 12.35, but that the officers did not at that point leave the vehicle. Perhaps they couldn't locate the cottage and took another turn around the block? This seems to be backed up by their alleged return at 12.41. At this point a man, claimed to be Battistelli, walked away from the car, perhaps trying to find the cottage on foot, returning again and heading over to the cottage gate at 12.48. The actual arrival time is, they say, 12.58 due to a ten-minute discrepancy in the CCTV clock. This is proven as a *Carabinieri* officer is seen arriving at 1.32pm, when phone records show that a call was received from the apparently lost officer asking for directions at 1.29pm. Therefore, they say, the clock must be inaccurate. This theory is further backed up by the fact that the *Polizia Postale* at no point report that they saw or heard Raffaele making any calls to the *Carabinieri* or indeed anyone else.

Whatever time they were called, the *Carabinieri* did head to No. 7, Via della Pergola that day, eventually arriving at around 1.30pm just after the *Squadra Mobile*, who had apparently been called by Battistelli following the discovery of Meredith's body. Seeing that they were in attendance, they left them to deal with whatever was happening inside the cottage. Some say this was carefully orchestrated by Raffaele to avoid the *Carabinieri* becoming involved, some that they simply got lost on the way and arrived late.

Mobile phone records may not be able to prove what's going on in the mind of the caller, but they can certainly be interpreted to build up an idea of their movements and motivations and can, in certain circumstances, place people in a certain geographical area, with varying degrees of accuracy. A high proportion of the discussions about this case revolve around mobile phone use; quite apart from the question of when the *Polizia Postale* arrived, a whole series of phone calls from around midday onwards has also been put under the spotlight. For example, what were the specific timings of Amanda's calls to Filomena following her discovery at the cottage and do they imply a sinister motive?

Going back to the night before Meredith was discovered, phone records show that the couple turned their phones off on the night of 1 November; Amanda at 8.35pm and Raffaele at 8.42pm. The following morning Raffaele's first phone activity was an incoming text message from his father at 06.02am, the assumption being that this is when Raffaele turned his phone back on. Amanda did not use her phone until 12.07pm when she tried to call Meredith's phone, followed by a call to Filomena. In quick succession she then called both of Meredith's phones again, and then followed three incoming calls from Filomena. At 12.47pm she placed a call to her mother in Seattle.

Simply put, these calls can either be construed as a means of Amanda creating an alibi for herself, or they represent her trying to work out what on earth was going on in the cottage and frantically trying to place Meredith's whereabouts. Amanda's timeline does not quite tally with the phone records but whether this is simply a matter of not remembering the exact sequence of events, or if there is a more sinister reason behind it is of course up for debate. For example, she does not specify times but says that the first call she placed was to her mother in Seattle, while she was on her way back from the cottage to Raffaele's. Edda told her to call her flatmates, so her subsequent phone call was to Filomena while at Raffaele's house. On Filomena's advice she then tried to call Meredith on her British phone, followed by her Italian phone. She says that Filomena then called her back while she was at Raffaele's apartment, following which she returned with him to the cottage. At this point she took another call from Filomena to find out what was going on. Her next call was to her mother.

The actual phone records reflect slightly differently; the first call placed was at 12.07pm to Meredith. She then called Filomena at 12.08pm. Following on from that call, she tried Meredith's phones again, first the Italian and then the British; the calls did not go through and lasted a matter of seconds. Filomena then called Amanda at 12.12pm, 12.20pm and 12.34pm. When Amanda answered at 12.20pm, she was still at Raffaele's house and by 12.34pm she answered at the cottage. At 12.47pm, Amanda placed the first phone call home to Seattle. Almost simultaneously, Raffaele was calling his sister at 12.50pm, followed by the *Carabinieri* at 12.51pm and 12.54pm.

What possible reason could Amanda have for allegedly lying about the order in which she made those calls? Some suggest that she placed those phone calls in order to create an alibi. The first phone call to Meredith (which Amanda does not mention in her statements or book) was to check if the phone (which she had stolen and thrown into the neighbour's garden) had yet been found. Why else would she not mention to Filomena that she had already tried the phone? Why would she ring the British phone and not the Italian one? And why did she only let those phones ring for three and four seconds if she was genuinely trying to locate her? Some speculate that there is an even more sinister motive at play here; that Amanda called Filomena with the sole purpose of setting her up to find the body, a plan disrupted by the surprise appearance of the *Polizia Postale*. This is backed up by the allegation that Amanda was lying, implying that she made that first call to Filomena from No. 7, Via della Pergola when records show that it was in fact made from Raffaele's house. Did Amanda want Filomena to return to the house first, knowing what she would find there?

The counter argument to this is the assertion that there's absolutely nothing sinister in Amanda trying to call Meredith and then subsequently calling Filomena and in fact if anything proves the opposite, that Amanda was genuinely worried about her and was trying to contact her straight away. The short phone calls of three or four seconds? The phone was not reachable at this point; it did not ring but went straight to the equivalent of answerphone. Getting the timings wrong? She was in a panic and can't be expected to remember the exact order in which she placed the calls while she was in such a state.

If the discussions about physical evidence can be ambiguous, those surrounding Amanda's behaviour and how it is interpreted are even more so. In contrast to analysing and interpreting actual data such as phone records, the other question forming in people's minds even at this point in the investigation was regarding Amanda's behaviour; in particular, why on earth did she take a shower in a room with bloodstains on the basin and shower mat?

Quite apart from the shower, the first red flag for many is that before Amanda even entered the house, she noticed that the front door was open. She admits that this 'should have rattled me more', but that it was easily explained as the 'old latch didn't catch unless we used a key', and thought perhaps that the wind had blown it open.[8] On a very basic level the argument about entering a house whose front door is open and then taking a shower despite discovering blood in the bathroom could be put down to a matter of personal hygiene; for some, the idea of walking into a bathroom, seeing blood on the shower mat and on the sink and then proceeding to take a shower is inconceivable. However, no matter how inappropriate many may find it, the truth is that some people would simply not be fazed by it; no matter how disgusting it may seem to some, to others it simply wouldn't bother them.

Amanda's version describes two 'pea sized flecks of blood' in the bathroom basin and another smear on the taps. The blood was dry, and she assumed it might be something to do with her recent ear piercing. She says she didn't notice the 'reddish-brown splotch the size of an orange' on the bathmat until she got out of the shower and put this down to potential menstrual issues of Meredith. It was only when she discovered the faeces in the other, larger, bathroom where she went to borrow Filomena's hair dryer, that she began to become alarmed and left the house with her 'heart banging painfully' in fear.[9]

On the face of it this is a plausible set of events, taking into account the fact that some people are simply more hyper-hygienic than others. For those who think she is lying, however, the whole set of circumstances becomes highly improbable. There's no denying that in photographs of the bathmat the 'reddish-brown splotch' clearly forms the shape of a footprint when viewed close up and from above. It's conceivable, however, that, at a glance, it may have resembled more of a shapeless splotch. But how could she possibly not have noticed it for what it was while stepping over it to get into the shower? Others are convinced that judging by the photographs of her snapped after the discovery of Meredith's body, she had not taken a shower that morning, rendering the whole shower story preposterous.

It Begins

Back at the crime scene, the *Squadra Mobile* team, including Detective Superintendent Monica Napoleoni (head of Perugia's homicide squad) and Inspector Stefano Buratti, arrived at around 1.30pm, followed shortly afterwards by their boss Marco Chiacchiera (deputy head of the *Squadra Mobile*). Soon afterwards an ambulance arrived at around 1.50pm followed by Perugia's forensic police. The investigation would now begin.

Public prosecutor for the magistrates, Giuliano Mignini, happened to be on twenty-four-hour call that week. As per procedure, Chiacchiera contacted him with the news that a woman's body had been found and fetched him back to the scene, where they returned at around 3.00pm. Here Mignini assessed the scene and drew his first conclusions about what had occurred; he immediately felt that the break-in had been staged, and that the fact that Meredith's body had been covered by a duvet meant the involvement of a female in the crime, or at the very least someone she knew. Mignini would become, and remains, a divisive character; on one hand ridiculed for his Sherlock Holmes-esque delusions of detective intuition, and on the other put on a pedestal as a brave and relentless searcher for the truth.

Luca Lalli, the forensic pathologist who had been summoned by the *Squadra Mobile*, was now also on site, alongside the forensic police who were by then examining the cottage and the crime scene itself. Mignini instructed Lalli to assess the body but to touch it as little as possible, allowing the forensic police to complete their investigations first. Lalli managed to establish that rigor mortis had set in but was then asked to clear the scene and wait for the elite forensic team, who were on their way from Rome, to arrive and continue the investigation in more detail. He did not get a chance to take the temperature of the body in order to establish time of death, which would of course prove contentious later on, particularly during the final appeal. In one documentary interview, Mignini insists that he did ask Lalli to take the temperature straight away but bowed to the wishes of the forensic police to wait until their investigation was complete. Whoever made the decision on site, the fact remains that Meredith's time of death could not be assessed with any strict accuracy at this point.

It wasn't until 8.00pm that evening that Patrizia Stefanoni from the elite forensic police in Rome arrived at the cottage and began her work. She discovered Meredith's white bra, which was soaked in blood and had had the left shoulder strap severed. The cloth and metal clasp had been cut off and was missing. She also discovered numerous bloodstains; the bedroom door handle was broken and smeared with blood and there were twenty bloodstains on a white cupboard door. On the inside of the open left-door of the cupboard, there was a bloody smear which appeared to have been made by fingers. There was another similar smear on the wall opposite and bloodstains on the lower part of the desk. In the bathroom where Amanda had showered, she found blood on the basin and tap, and on a box of cotton buds. There was also blood on the blue mat under the basin, on the bidet, the toilet lid, some floor tiles close to the toilet, the light switch and door frame.

It wasn't until gone midnight that Luca Lalli was allowed to examine the body. At this point, he discovered two wounds on the front and right of her neck, both about one inch long. On the left side of her neck there was a 'three-inch gaping wound',[1] which he surmised had been made by a knife, or possibly a piece of glass from the broken window. Meredith's body was removed at 1.30am for autopsy, at which point Lalli discovered the missing bra clasp under a cushion, which was in turn underneath Meredith's body. He pointed this out to the forensic police and left the scene.

Meredith's autopsy was carried out on 4 November, with the conclusion that the time of death had been around 11.00pm on 1 November. She had suffered twenty-three wounds in total; seven of them appeared to be made by a knife, and the others consisted of bruises. The cause of death was 'cardio-respiratory failure due to asphyxiation caused by an attempt to strangle or suffocate her, and to a subsequent haemorrhage from the biggest wound to the neck "caused by a pointed and cutting weapon"'.[2] In Lalli's opinion, 'someone held the girl from behind with his hands under her jawbone and she was then stabbed by someone standing in front of her.'[3]

In the meantime, back on the 2 November at around 3.00pm, the police gathered Filomena, Amanda and their boyfriends together and told them to head over to the *questura* (police station) to meet them there, where they would take their statements as to the events that morning. Amanda travelled with Raffaele, Luca and Paola, during which time they had a conversation about how Meredith had died, establishing among themselves that she had indeed been murdered, and that her throat had been cut. At around 1.45pm Filomena called Laura to tell her the news and she started to make her way back to Perugia from Rome. She then called Giacomo who was on a train heading back to Perugia with Stefano and broke the news to them both that Meredith was dead.

It appears that Meredith's British friends heard the news initially from the local radio which was reporting the discovery of a body just an hour after it had happened, following which a friend of Sophie Purton's from the student exchange office at the *Stranieri* called her at around 3.00pm to ask her if she had a friend named Meredith. She had heard rumours mentioning the name in connection with the discovery of a body, and while she tried to reassure Sophie that it probably wasn't the same Meredith, asked if it would be ok to pass her phone number onto the police. The friends had all been increasingly worried about Meredith that morning as she had missed her class, and none of them had been able to get hold of her. They decided to head back to the cottage, but in the meantime, Sophie received a call from the police asking her and her friends to head to the *Stranieri* where they would be picked up by a police car. At around 6.00pm the police arrived and escorted them to the *questura* to join Amanda and the others. Everything was now falling into place and the girls gradually came to the crushing realisation that they had been right to worry about Meredith.

The initial interviews took hours; by the time police had finished questioning Amanda, Raffaele and the others who had witnessed the discovery of the body, everyone else had also assembled at the *questura*: Sophie, Amy, Robyn, Natalie, Pisco, Laura and the boys from the downstairs flat. At around 3.00am Amanda and the British girls were taken to be fingerprinted. According to her, she left the *questura* at around 5.30am with Raffaele, Laura, Filomena, Giacomo and the 'other guys from downstairs'.[4] Raffaele says that Amanda was questioned firstly in Italian and then with an interpreter, during which she went through the events of that morning, after which she had her fingerprints taken. He also gave a statement; they were allowed to leave at 5.30am on 3 November and told to return later that morning at 11.00am.

After this initial round of interviews it was clear that, having all been out of town at the time of the murder, the boys from the downstairs basement were eliminated of any suspicion, as were Filomena and Laura. Meredith's British friends were also not under suspicion, and they all made plans to head back to England as soon as possible. In fact, Amy and Robyn headed for the airport and went home on 3 November. Sophie also wanted to leave, but her parents had already booked themselves a flight to Perugia to come and fetch her.

There was also no reason to think that any of the others on the periphery of the friendship group that had been questioned, for example Pisco, had anything whatsoever to do with the murder. Suspicion was beginning to fall on those closest to Meredith who had the potential means to have been involved – especially given Mignini's initial thought that this was an inside job. As all of the other flatmates were in the clear, the prosecutor's gaze was now firmly aimed at Amanda and Raffaele.

Although there is a feeling that Mignini was laser focused on the couple right from the beginning to the detriment of any other lines of enquiry, other avenues were being investigated at this point; several names had come up during the statements given by the group. First, the girls' Moroccan friend Shaky, perhaps flagged up due to the intimidating behaviour he had expressed previously. Second, the boys from the downstairs flat were asked about recent visitors to the cottage and when questioned, confirmed that one had been a young man nicknamed 'The Baron', who they thought was a South African and who by some accounts had been strongly attracted to Amanda. He would of course turn out to be Rudy Guede, but his identity for the moment would remain a mystery to the boys and investigators.

So, at the very outset of the investigation, before the forensic police arrived and even before these statements had been taken, what did the police have to go on? Simply put and taken on face value, they found a cottage with its front door open. They found some evidence of blood in one bathroom and faeces in another. They encountered a locked bedroom door, and evidence of a break-in in the room next door.

And then, they discovered a body. Inevitably events then snowballed, but one of the first questions which crossed the minds of the investigators, and indeed is still debated hotly to this day, is how did the perpetrator get in and out of the house that night? Was he/she let in by Meredith or another occupant of the house? Or was the motive initially burglary, and did the murderer break into No. 7, Via della Pergola? To answer this, one must ask a subsequent question: was the break-in that was discovered in Filomena's room real, or staged?

To simplify, there are generally two opinions about the answer to this question. First, the assertion that the burglary was staged. This is put forward by those who think that Amanda, Raffaele and Rudy (or some combination of the three) were responsible for Meredith's murder. In this scenario, after the event and in an attempt to cover up after themselves, they broke the window in Filomena's room from the inside to make it look like a robbery had occurred and fled the scene.

The alternative scenario is that this was an authentic burglary attempt and generally the opinion of those who believe Rudy acted alone; he planned to burgle the house and threw the rock against the window to ascertain if anyone was in. When no lights came on and no one appeared to look for the source of the noise he scaled the wall and let himself in, making himself at home until Meredith unexpectedly returned, whereupon he killed her. Despite initially thinking that nothing had been taken from the cottage, detectives did later discover that 300 euros belonging to Meredith, which she had withdrawn to pay her rent, were missing from her room. Detectives were also unable to locate her wallet, and of course her two mobile phones had also been stolen, albeit then abandoned. Rudy would later claim that Meredith told him she thought Amanda had stolen her rent money, but whoever took it, it was never recovered.

In the meantime, though, was the burglary staged or not? The answer essentially boils down again to two further questions: could Rudy (or for that matter, anyone at all) have physically scaled the exterior wall to access Filomena's window, and was the position of the glass inside the room consistent with the large stone having been thrown from the outside in order to gain entry.

First then, how accessible was the window? Those who dismiss the break-in theory are adamant that the choice of window as the most convenient access point into the house simply does not ring true given the potential to be seen from the road – but more importantly, they say that it is improbable, if not impossible, for someone to climb up and enter the house through that particular window. In fact, it has been proven with varying degrees of success, not least by Raffaele's lawyer during the first trial, that it was *possible* to enter the house in that way, but the assertion is that just because it's *possible*, doesn't mean that it's *probable*. Yes, Rudy could possibly have scaled the wall and gained access, but why choose a window which is demonstrably difficult to get to? Another point that strengthens this argument is that the exterior was completely clean; given that it had been raining that night, surely Rudy would have left muddy marks behind as he scrabbled up towards Filomena's window.

Those who believe that Rudy broke in through the window argue that it's perfectly possible to do so, particularly for an athletic man like him, and that the worry about being seen is a moot point. Yes, there is a main road running alongside the cottage from which the window can be seen, but some argue that at that time of night the darkness and its position renders it virtually in shadow and therefore an ideal point of entry. Perhaps a stronger argument is the assertion that Rudy had been known to use this same method to break into several houses in the past, right down to the throwing of rocks, and the scaling of walls.

Coming to the second question then; what about the position of the glass in Filomena's bedroom?

Most accounts agree that Amanda, Raffaele and Battistelli checked out Filomena's bedroom together when the *Polizia Postale* arrived and found what appeared to be evidence of a break-in; there was glass on the floor by the window, and a large stone or rock under the window or by Filomena's desk chair, half in and half out of a torn paper bag. The big debate is whether or not the glass was on top of the pile of clothes lying under the window; if so, it would indicate that it had been broken after the room had been ransacked, indicating an attempt at staging. Some accounts allude to Battistelli being dubious about the validity of the break-in from the offset, and Mignini certainly believed that it had been staged from the moment he arrived.

However, some accounts say that there was glass on top of and underneath various clothes and items in the room and suggest that the inadequate crime scene photographs do not accurately prove that the glass was discovered on top only. They also argue that at least four people searched through Filomena's room looking for evidence of things being stolen before the cottage was finally sealed off as a crime scene, and even afterwards Filomena was able to pop back in to grab her laptop and other belongings after Meredith's body was found. Therefore, it is perfectly possible that things may have been moved during this time. It would certainly not be the last time that accusations of shoddy crime scene management leading to possible contamination would be put forward.

One last factor which may affect the direction of the glass from the window is the matter of whether or not the shutters on the window were open or closed. There was some evidence of glass grouping in the windowsill, suggesting that the window was broken from the inside, with the closed shutter preventing it from falling outside and onto the floor below. No glass was found outside the window on the floor below, indicating that the shutters were probably closed when the glass was broken. The counter argument is that the shutters were open, therefore the glass fell inwards on impact hence the grouping in the sill, and the lack of glass on the outside of the building.

There are other issues, of course; initially nothing of value appeared to have been taken from the room or indeed from anywhere throughout the whole cottage. Even this fact is interpreted in two different ways; either it was clearly staged, otherwise the burglar would have stolen something, or it was clearly not staged, as anyone wishing to convince the police that a burglary had taken place would have made every effort to remove at least one item of value.

Suspicion

Although doubts were beginning to creep in about some of the physical evidence such as that surrounding the break-in, most people agree that it was Amanda and Raffaele's objectively odd behaviour in the days following the murder that first drew attention to them and placed them firmly in the role of suspects. They were seen kissing and caressing each other while standing outside the cottage after Meredith's body was discovered, and spotted on the 3 November buying underwear and joking together. Amanda would sit on his lap or sprawl over him while waiting at the *questura* to be interviewed and later in the process she was allegedly seen turning cartwheels in the same place.

It's hard to argue against the fact that, whether or not Amanda had anything to do with the murder, her actions over the following days drew a negative reaction from those around her. Possibly the most damning and caught on camera for all the world to see, were her and Raffaele's public displays of affection. Kissing and cuddling at the scene of the crime, lounging on each other in the waiting room at the *questura*, laughing and making silly faces at each other while the rest of the girls appeared much more upset.

These apparently inappropriate actions would come back to haunt the pair; Meredith's friends recall them loudly kissing at the *questura*, making smacking noises with their lips, Amanda curled up on Raffaele's lap nuzzled 'like a koala bear', and even he, retrospectively, found that her behaviour made him 'uneasy' – although at the time he didn't feel the need to draw attention to it.[1] Perhaps feeling the need to distance himself somewhat, he explains in his book that the quirky behaviour which had at first drawn him to her now seemed out of place and childish, and that he was beginning to understand why Meredith's friends were not particularly keen on her.

Other alarm bells began to ring for the investigators, with one of the first being an alleged slip up on Amanda's part; she told her mother on the phone that, despite not being able to see into the room at the time of the discovery, Meredith's body had been found in front of her wardrobe in her bedroom. In fact, she'd been found in the middle of her room covered with her duvet, and investigators would later theorise that Meredith had been killed in front of her wardrobe, and then dragged to the centre of the room after her death.

This led to speculation; how would Amanda have known about the original position of the body, if she hadn't witnessed the discovery of the body and hadn't been in the room when the murder took place? This is a major scoring point for those who think she was, in fact, in the room during the murder. Amanda has an explanation. She heard several shouts from the people who discovered the body – 'a foot!' 'Blood!' and '*armadio*' (armoire, or closet). With these three things in her mind, she imagined the scene: 'a faceless body stuffed in the armoire, a foot sticking out', and she relayed this thought process to her mother – 'they've found a body near the cupboard or in the cupboard, I can't make out which'.[2]

There is also dispute about whether Amanda relayed the information that Meredith had died by having her throat cut before this particular piece of news had been released, and it caused alarm not just because she knew the information, but perhaps more because of the way in which she delivered it. On the face of it though, it seems that Amanda was not the only person to have discovered the cause of death. After the body was found, Luca and Paola were trying to 'read lips and overhear' what the police were saying, with Luca subsequently telling Raffaele that he had heard or seen the police say that 'the victim's throat has been slashed'.[3] During the car ride to the *questura*, he imparted this information to Amanda and Raffaele.

However, on Sophie's arrival at the police station Amanda informed her that '[Meredith's] throat was cut and then she was put in a cupboard,' in a 'flat and matter-of-fact tone'. Later, when chatting to Meredith's British friends, Natalie expressed the hope that she didn't suffer to which Amanda replied, 'What do you think? They cut her throat, Natalie. She fucking bled to death!'[4]

Amanda and Raffaele explain it differently. Amanda says at the police station that, 'trying to be helpful, I shared the information I had, much of which turned out to be wrong'. She says of her interaction with Natalie that she was incredibly worked up and enraged about the murder, that she was by her own admission 'angry and blunt', and that what she said to Natalie was 'how could she not of suffered? She got her fucking throat slit. Fucking bastards.[*sic*]'[5]

Meredith's friends found Amanda's general attitude surprising and unsympathetic in the days following; she was concerned about where she would live and whether she would get her rent back, but didn't direct any of this concern towards her murdered flatmate. In fact, Meredith's friend Sophie recalls Amanda speculating that the worst thing about this whole nightmare was that if she had been at home the previous night, it could have happened to her. And more questions were beginning to be asked: why did it take so long for her and Raffaele to contact the police? Why did she have a mop with her when the police turned up? On Monday, 5 November, Amanda was back at her lectures at 9.00am which did not sit well with some fellow students, and on that same evening, she and Raffaele did not attend the candlelight vigil which had been arranged in memory of Meredith.

The investigation continued, and over the next few days everyone involved would be subject to further interviews by the police. According to some reports, after their initial interview Amanda was taken back to the cottage by Napoleoni and Mignini on 3 November and interviewed again that afternoon back at the station, which slightly contradicts Amanda and Raffaele's account that they were both called back at 11.00am that day having only left the *questura* at around 5.30am. However, Amanda's account is that during that trip to the cottage on 3 November she and investigators visited the boys' room downstairs, where they discovered a blood-stained comforter in Stefano's room alongside his crop of marijuana plants. The blood on the comforter would later turn out to be feline, from an injured cat.

As would become a recurring theme, Amanda certainly didn't help herself over the course of the next few days. First, on 4 November, she sent a long, rambling email to various family and friends in Seattle. On the face of it, the purpose was to reassure them that she was fine in herself and to explain what had happened to her over the past few days. It's almost 3,000 words long and doesn't contain a single paragraph break or capital letter. It's littered with spelling mistakes which would imply that it was written quickly and with little regard for accuracy; there's barely any punctuation and it reads as a pure stream of consciousness. On one 'pro-Amanda' website, it's presented having been neatened up – spellings and grammar have been corrected and the whole thing has been made much easier to read by splitting it up into paragraphs. On a 'pro-guilt' website, it is presented in its original, rambling form; the first presents a coherent explanation by an innocent victim, the other a panicked ramble written by someone trying to put forward her version of events before the facts became public. No matter how it's presented though, the content is at best confusing and at worst full of red flags. Amanda does herself no favours here, but arguably she had never expected the email to become public, not having anticipated it being forwarded to the police in Seattle and then on to investigators in Perugia. She certainly comes across as unfeeling and selfish, not least when she complains that 'it kind of sucks that we have to pay the next month's rent.[6]

The idea that this email was sent as a kind of insurance against future accusations could seem to be substantiated by certain phrases (or their interpretation). For example, why did she feel the need to let everyone know that Meredith had put some washing on that day? (Some theories suggest that, as the washing machine was found to contain a mixture of Amanda's and Meredith's recently washed clothes, it had somehow been used as part of the alleged clean-up and it seems an innocuous thing to mention.) Also, that she had grabbed a mop to clean up the spill at Raffaele's, that she had gone out to buy underwear, or the order in which she had called Meredith's phones? She gives a brief explanation of the different types of police force in Italy and is sure to assert that they called the police, and goes on to describe the evidence of a break-in. Arguably, these would all become pieces of circumstantial evidence or behaviours that many believe point to her guilt, so was she simply setting up her story ahead of time?

She also makes sure to explain the circumstances in which she put together her image of Meredith's body in the room:

> we checked the houe out, talked to the poli,a nd in a big they all opened merediths door. i was in the kitchen stadning aside, have really done my part for the situation but when they opened merediths door and i heard filomena scream 'a foot! a foot!' in italian i immedaitely tried to get to merediths foom but raffael grabbed me and took me out of the house.[*sic*]⁷

On the other hand, was this email simply a method by which to relieve her stress, to get it off her chest before she forgets any details which may become important later? She writes: 'id like to get it all out and not have to repeat myself a hundred times like ive been having to do at the police station'.[*sic*]⁸

It's important to remember that the first iPhone had only been unveiled in June of that year and the world of free international calls via WhatsApp were a luxury of the future. Calling home was incredibly expensive, so it's completely feasible that someone, particularly one as verbose as Amanda, would want to collate all of this information in one place, and release it out to as many people as possible in one fell swoop. She does request that it doesn't get into the hands of journalists by explaining: 'id like to ssay that I was strictly told not to speak about this, but im speaking with you people who are not involved and cant do anything bad except talk to journalists, which I hope you wont do' [*sic*],[9] and it's still not entirely clear why the former owner of a bar where she worked in Seattle forwarded it on to the police, but one can imagine two scenarios leading to this decision. One, that he thought it contained information which would be useful for the police investigation and two, that within those scrambled words he saw some element that alarmed him. In the same way that Meredith's friends had thought her initial reaction to the situation was strange, perhaps this email triggered some red flags for at least one recipient. Either way, Amanda says she 'wrote it quickly, without a lot of thought',[10] and pressed send at around 3.45am of 4 November.

Amanda, Filomena and Laura were all called back to the *questura* later that day for a further round of interviews. As on every other occasion, Raffaele accompanied Amanda, which by some accounts was starting to annoy the police; he was not required to be there himself, could she not go anywhere without him tagging along? The counter argument is of course simple, she was a foreigner with a basic knowledge of the language and with her family support network over 5,000 miles away she did not want to be alone.

Prosecutors became more suspicious of Amanda and Raffaele when they discovered that their phones had become inactive at almost exactly the same time on the night of the murder, indicating that they had been deliberately switched off together. The issue of the phones has also become a talking point over the years; did they switch their phones off on the evening of the murder until the following morning and if so, what are the implications of those actions? It's clear from phone records that Amanda and Raffaele's phones were turned off, or at the very least not used, from around 8.45pm on the night of the murder, until around 6.00am (Raffaele) and around 12.00pm (Amanda) on the following day. Raffaele's last activity had been a call from his father at 8.42pm the previous evening and Amanda's had been her text message to Patrick at 8.35pm.

This sequence of events broadly indicates two different motivations. First, that the couple turned their phones off at this point in order not to be disturbed during the planned murder of Meredith. Some have suggested that the phones were turned off as they were planning to meet up with someone, perhaps Rudy, in town to initiate a drugs deal.

The other alternative is that the couple, once they realised that they had no further obligations that evening after Patrick had told Amanda not to worry about coming into work, and Raffaele was no longer required to help his friend with her mother's luggage pick-up, they decided that they did not want to be disturbed and settled down to watch *Amelie*.

Either way, on the back of this knowledge the police bugged the waiting room at the *questura* where the couple would sit talking together and put a tap on both of their phones. No game-changing confessions were overheard during these conversations, but various reports say that Amanda was heard to tell Raffaele that 'I can't take it anymore',[11] and that she was also heard talking about an unknown man whom the police at that point assumed was the killer, convincing them that she was protecting someone. Other reports say that she was talking about Shaky and his creepy behaviour, as he had already been flagged up as a possible person of interest. He would eventually be eliminated from enquiries.

Following their interviews on 4 November, Napoleoni took the female flatmates back to the cottage where they were to meet up with Mignini. The purpose of the visit, they were told, was that they wanted to clarify if any of their knives were missing from the kitchen in an attempt to try to establish the whereabouts of the murder weapon and they confirmed that no, nothing was missing. This caused Amanda, by her own admission, to have a panic attack, with the sudden realisation that the police were 'asking me to pick out what might have been used to slash Meredith's throat'.[12] It was becoming too overwhelming to bear. Mignini would go on to assert that he believed she was reliving the murder in her own mind when she put her hands over her ears and screamed that day, an action brought on by horror and guilt at what she had done or witnessed on 1 November.

Sophie was interviewed again on 5 November, with police looking for more detail about the male visitors who had previously visited the cottage. Again, Shaky was discussed along with the 'South African man' they had heard about from the boys downstairs. Sophie reiterated that she did not recall Meredith meeting the South African in the days running up to the murder. Raffaele was also called back on that same evening and, mirroring Amanda's earlier lone interviews, she accompanied him to the station even though she was not required to do so, having nowhere else to go and nothing else to do. After being summoned by police, Raffaele didn't arrive at the station until around 10.30pm that evening. He felt that it was reasonable for him to be allowed to finish his meal first, the police felt otherwise, irritated at his arrogance by deliberately keeping them waiting. Either way, this late interrogation would prove to be a major turning point for him, Amanda, and indeed for the whole investigation. As yet there was no physical evidence against the pair, but by the early hours of 6 November, they would both be under arrest.

And this turning point would be that during Raffaele's interrogation, which lasted until around 1.00am on 6 November, he changed his story; on the night of 1 November, he now said, he had been with Amanda at her cottage in the afternoon when they saw Meredith together. However, by 9.00pm he was now home alone as Amanda had headed off to Le Chic to meet some friends and had not returned until 1.00am. He said the following morning, Amanda had headed back to her cottage at around 10.00am and returned to his at around 11.30am, with tales of the strange things she had discovered there: the open door, the blood, the faeces. When asked why he had changed his story, he replied: 'I told you a lot of bullshit in my earlier statement, because she'd convinced me that her version of what happened was right, and I didn't think of the inconsistencies'.[13]

As is so familiar now with this case, the next sequence of events is muddy and contradictory, but essentially boils down to Amanda's word against the police as to what happened during her interrogation, which ran concurrently with Raffaele's, and again, different spins lead to very different conclusions about the events surrounding what Amanda said and did, and the accusations she made during the night. Her recollection is that at around 11.00pm a 'silver haired officer' spoke to her informally as she was waiting for Raffaele, asking for her help in establishing the identity of potential visitors or suspects at the cottage, and it was then that she 'suddenly remembered Rudy Guede for the first time'.[14]

This was also the point at which she chose to try and relax with some stretching exercises. This seemingly innocuous behaviour, albeit objectively inappropriate for the occasion, would become one of the major issues in the ongoing analysis of Amanda's behaviour, and arguably the image of her turning cartwheels in the police waiting room may have been even more damaging to her reputation than her and Raffaele's shared kiss at the scene of the crime. Was this behaviour simply Amanda's way of relaxing, or does it show a complete lack of respect against the backdrop of a murder investigation?

The cartwheel story is perhaps one of the most memorable events to be reported in the press during the investigation. The British tabloid press in particular made much of this, with headlines in *The Mirror* claiming, rather misleadingly, that, 'Meredith Kercher murder accused turned cartwheels and performed the splits immediately after Meredith Kercher killing', going on to say that 'the woman accused of murdering British student Meredith Kercher performed a series of bizarre gymnastic stunts in front of puzzled detectives immediately after the killing'.[15] Misleading certainly by describing these actions as having taken place 'immediately' after the killing, rather than the truth that this incident happened on 5 November, four days after Meredith was killed. It's clear that this type of reporting imprinted this behaviour in the minds of the public much more solidly than perhaps it should have.

Nevertheless, many people deem her actions inappropriate, whether or not they believe her to have been involved in Meredith's murder. Supporters stress that performing some simple yoga exercises to calm herself down during an incredibly stressful situation is perfectly normal behaviour. Amanda herself plays down the whole scenario, explaining that she was simply doing some stretches and 'touched my toes, flexed my quads, extended my arms overhead',[16] and only proceeded to do the splits after one of the police officers commented on how flexible she was and asked her to demonstrate her yoga skills.

Other accounts explain in more detail that it was Napoleoni who spotted her 'doing the splits followed by a cartwheel', and that later detectives 'saw her do the yoga bridge position, lying on the floor on her back with her knees up, hands at her side, and arching her back upwards several times as she took slow, deep breaths'.[17] She was reprimanded and told in no uncertain terms that a police station was no place for practicing yoga.

Whatever the level of exertion, according to Amanda, at this point Officer Rita Ficarra walked in to witness this impromptu yoga session and, when she realised that Amanda and the officer present were discussing the case, suggested that they ought to get themselves into a more formal setting and put what she was saying down on record. She was taken to a separate room, at which point she was told that they had sent for an interpreter who, she says, arrived at about 12.30am. Before this, she was peppered with relentless questions and was starting to feel exhausted and confused. Once the interpreter arrived the room became crowded, with several different officers coming and going throughout the interrogation. The break came when Napoleoni popped her head round the door to deliver the (for Amanda) devastating news that Raffaele had changed his story. Amanda had not been with him that night, he now said, in fact she had asked him to lie for her. He had whipped her alibi away from her and she was now on her own.

After this bombshell, the officers suddenly introduced Amanda's boss at Le Chic, Patrick Lumumba, into the equation. They took her phone and showed her their proof via text that she had arranged to meet up with him that night ('*Ci vediamo piu tardi bonna serata!*' 'See you later!')[18] Ficarra slapped her over the head to get her attention, continually asking who this man was, and why she had arranged to meet him later that night. She was threatened with prison unless she helped them and eventually she snapped, just to get them to stop with the relentless pressure.

By 1.45am she had signed a piece of paper they gave to her containing a statement written in Italian, confirming that she had in fact told Raffaele she was going to work, but instead had met Patrick at the basketball courts and from there they made their way to the cottage. Following on from her initial text she received from Patrick, the statement proffers that:

> I answered [the message from Patrick] straight away, and then I left the house telling my boyfriend that I had to go to work. I have to say that in the afternoon Raffaele and I had smoked a joint and so I felt confused because

I don't often use either light or heavy drugs. I met Patrick just afterwards at the basketball court on Piazza Grimana and I went home with him. I don't remember whether Meredith was already there or whether she arrived a short time later. It's hard for me to remember but Patrick had sex with Meredith, he was infatuated with her, but I don't remember if Meredith was threatened first. I remember confusedly that he's the one that killed her.[19]

Once Amanda had signed this statement, Mignini arrived. In answer to her request for a lawyer, his response was, 'it will only make it worse'. She didn't need one, he assured her. Following a further interrogation with Mignini present, at 5.45am she signed another statement confessing her presence in the cottage on the night of the murder and naming Patrick as the person who had killed Meredith. 'I cannot recall how much time they stayed together in the room but can only say that at a certain point I heard Meredith screaming and I, frightened, covered my ears. Then I don't remember anything anymore, I am very confused in my head.' She also admitted that she was 'not sure if Raffaele was there or not', landing him firmly in the role of fellow suspect, effectively cancelling out each other's alibis.[20]

As Amanda tells it, she was still under the impression that by telling them about Patrick and signing the statement she was simply helping the police with their enquiries, desperate to please, doing as she was told and agreeing to whatever it was that they wanted to hear in order to keep them happy. She had fallen into an exhausted half sleep, curled up in a chair in the interrogation room when she suddenly awoke in a panic that what she had put her signature to was wrong, misremembered and would do more harm than good to the investigation in the long run. She must put it right. She wanted to help. 'I needed to say that I had doubts about what I'd signed, to let the police know they couldn't rely on my declarations as the truth.'[21]

She asked Ficarra for paper and a pen, and hand wrote what she described as her '*memoriale*'. Much like the email she had written a few days previously, it was long and rambling and in it she tried to describe what had really happened that night in order to help the police. She starts with: 'This is very strange, I know, but really what happened is as confusing to me as it is to everyone else.' She goes on to assert that:

> In regards to this 'confession' that I made last night, I want to make it very clear that I'm very doubtful of the verity of my statements because they were made under the pressure of stress, shock and extreme exhaustion. Not only was I told I would be arrested and put in jail for thirty years, but I was also hit in the head when I didn't remember a fact correctly.
>
> However, it was under this pressure and after many hours of confusion that my mind came up with these answers. In my mind I saw Patrik [sic] in flashes of blurred images. I saw him near the basketball court. I saw him at my front door. I saw myself cowering in the kitchen with my hands over my ears because in my head I could hear Meredith screaming. But I've said this many times so as to make myself clear: these things seem unreal to me, like a dream, and I am unsure if they are real things that happened or are just dreams my head has made to try to answer the questions in my head and the questions I am being asked.[22]

Whatever positive outcome Amanda was expecting to occur after handing this over to police, it did not materialise; she was immediately arrested. Patrick had already been picked up from his home shortly after she had signed her statement at 1.45am and had been brought back to a holding cell at the *questura*.

Broadly, the sequence of events is more or less agreed on by everyone; Amanda started an informal chat with an officer at around 11.00pm during which she helped the police by again naming any male visitors to the house over the past few weeks. Following this, she was more formally interviewed, eventually with an interpreter present, and at some point, accused Patrick, after which she signed her first statement at around 1.45am. Sometime after this Mignini arrived and was present when she dictated her second statement which was completed at around 5.45am. Then followed her *memoriale*, and her arrest alongside Patrick and Raffaele.

The dispute lies in her treatment at the hands of the police, boiling down to three main points. Was she given anything to eat and drink? Was she offered a lawyer? And lastly, was she hit over the head? Amanda says absolutely no to the first two, and very definitely yes to the last.

By her account she had nothing to eat or drink for the entirety of the interrogation. Investigators say that they repeatedly fetched her snacks and camomile tea, to the point where the constant pandering began to irritate Napoleoni. With regards to the lawyer, Amanda says she was told she didn't need one, Mignini says he offered but she refused. Mignini asserts that when he entered the room, he explained to Amanda that, by law, he was not allowed to ask her questions but would simply take down her statement for her, pointing out anything she now said could be used against her. Therefore, he says, he told her at this point that she was entitled to a lawyer. Amanda, he says, refused, stating that she didn't need one. Simply put, one of them is not telling the truth.

The accusation of violence against the police is an altogether more serious matter, for which Amanda's parents would later be sued. Her narrative and that of her supporters, is that she was interrogated for hours by sometimes up to ten people at a time and hit across the head by officers when her answers were not satisfactory. The alternative narrative is that she was questioned by two or three officers, strongly yet fairly. The moment it all changed, they say, was when she was shown the message she had sent to Patrick, which had previously been deleted from her phone. The shock that this message had been discovered and thrown back at her caused an almost total collapse; she hunched her shoulders and started crying, 'It's him! I can hear it!'[23]

And here is where the problem lies, for everyone involved. This interrogation was not recorded either visually on video, or verbally on tape. And so, it is a matter of fact that what happened in that room will always come down to 'he said, she said'. And ultimately, this may well become the single most important factor in the outcome of this case.

For Amanda and Raffaele at least, things would go from bad to worse from now on with the discovery of the alleged murder weapon and potentially the first real piece of evidence placing the couple at the scene. Following the dramas of the previous night Raffaele had been escorted back to his apartment, accompanied by various officers including Finzi and Chiacchiera. According to Raffaele's account Finzi, he says, opened a drawer in the kitchen containing numerous knives and simply picked up the 'first knife that came to hand', asking Chiacchiera 'Will this knife do?' receiving the answer, 'Yes, yes it's great.'[24]

Finzi would later assert that he picked it because of his 'investigative intuition',[25] but does confirm that he chose this knife, and this knife alone, despite there being others beneath it in the drawer. Some accounts say that it was chosen because it looked particularly clean, as though it had been recently scrubbed. Interestingly, no other accounts mention the fact that Raffaele was present in his apartment when the knife was discovered, but all agree officers reported a strong smell of bleach on arrival. For investigators this was clear evidence of a clean-up, Raffaele puts it down to his maid having recently cleaned the apartment with the product Lysoform, as was her habit.

Raffaele's computer was also seized as evidence during this search, as were some Japanese manga comics, whose contents apparently contained a mix of violence and pornography which was commented on at the time by the officers who discovered them. Amanda's diary was also seized during a search of her room at No. 7, Via della Pergola. On Raffaele's arrival back at the *questura* with his fellow arrestees, all three of them were publicly taken from there to Capanne prison in a blaze of flashing camera bulbs.

A press conference swiftly followed, during which Police Chief Arturo De Felice triumphantly told the waiting reporters that they had arrested three people, and that Meredith had 'died fighting off a sexual attack, launched by a trio of friends'. When asked what the motive was, he replied that it was 'sexual, very much so'.[26]

So, on the face of it, case closed.

One Black Man for Another

Amanda and Raffaele were initially kept in custody based on the evidence of the knife which had been found, the fact that they both repeatedly changed their stories, and that Amanda's message to Patrick had seemed to imply that she was arranging to meet him later on, alongside her signed statement to that effect. The police needed more to go on though, of course.

As expected, more forensic evidence emerged over the following days but most notably, and what arguably took the investigation in a completely different direction, was the discovery of what some describe as 'the fourth suspect'.[1] On 15 November, the forensics team made another breakthrough, discovering a fragment of a bloody handprint on the cushion at the crime scene which did not belong to any of the suspects currently held in custody. On checking their records, they seem to have hit gold; on 16 November it was identified as belonging to Rudy Guede, the 'South African' visitor mentioned by the boys downstairs. They also found his DNA on the vaginal swab taken from Meredith and toilet paper from the unflushed toilet. They found his blood mixed with Meredith's on a shoulder bag and her sweatshirt. A fourth suspect, indeed.

So where was Rudy, and what was his story? Well, he was nowhere to be found, but it is indicative of the weight of importance placed on each of the suspects that the story of how and when Rudy was eventually detained seemed to hold much less interest, certainly in the press at the time, than the events surrounding Amanda and Raffaele. He had in fact fled to Germany and in one of the more sensationalised accounts of his departure, he had apparently 'crossed two borders, passed through the alps and evaded police in three countries',[2] before arriving, the account describes a tortured soul, haunted by the sight of a murdered girl whom he had been unable to help.

On 18 November the police announced a world-wide manhunt and Rudy would see pictures of himself splashed all over the news in Germany. Investigators used his Facebook account to try and trace any friends who might have been in touch and succeeded in contacting his childhood friend Giacomo Benedetti, asking for his help in contacting the fugitive. On 19 November he finally made contact via MSN messenger, and during this three-hour conversation, monitored by the police, Rudy told his story. According to him, he and Meredith had started to have consensual sexual contact on the night of 1 November but that he had been 'in the bathroom having a shit'[3] when the attack on Meredith had occurred. On fleeing the bathroom to find out what the disturbance was he bumped into a young Italian man who, on clocking Rudy, had blurted out something along the lines of 'black man found, culprit found',[4] and swiftly left the cottage leaving him, helpless, with a wounded Meredith.

What followed would become a point of contention in Raffaele and Amanda's final appeal, but the issue of subtleties of meaning being lost in translation plays a part here – inevitable given the multicultural and linguistic nature of the case. For supporters, this conversation is critical, in that Rudy does not at this stage mention Raffaele by name, and specifically states that Amanda did not have anything to do with the crime, and nor did Patrick. He did, however, imply that although the man he bumped into was not Patrick, he *may* have been Raffaele. His response to the question of whether he saw Amanda in the room was simple; '*Amanda non c'entra*'.[5] This can translate as: 'Amanda has nothing to do with this', or 'Amanda was not involved', whereas on some forums users will translate it as 'forget Amanda', which of course has a much more flexible meaning, open to interpretation. For many this should really be a moot point, however. The contention arises as Rudy was allowed to consistently change his story unchallenged throughout the investigation, which seems incredible given his fast-track trial excused him from being required to give evidence in Amanda and Raffaele's case therefore rendering them unable to challenge his story in any way. While on the run in Germany Rudy also, of course, had free access to every news report on the case, leaving him able to simply make up a story to fit the facts, if he so wished. Importantly for Amanda and Raffaele, his initial confirmation of her lack of involvement was forgotten.

During their contact, Giacomo persuaded his friend to head back to Milan by train to face the music, and the Italian police headed to the border at speed in the hopes that they would be able to arrest him as he entered the country. They were never able to have their moment of glory however; on 20 November he was picked up on a German train for not having a valid ticket, the warrant for his arrest flagged up and he was then taken to a prison in Koblenz. Here he repeated the same, but more detailed, account of what happened on the night of the 1 November.

And so it was that by 20 November, Patrick Lumumba had been released; the police had found no evidence to suggest that he was involved, and he was shown to have a watertight alibi; a Swiss professor who had been sitting with him in the bar during the time the murder took place. His false accusation at the hands of Amanda would go on to be one of the most crucial in the ultimate outcome of this case but for now, he was free to go.

Some, inevitably, take the stance that this treatment of Patrick, and indeed of Rudy, was deeply rooted in racism. The Italian papers at the time spoke of 'one black for another',[6] and Rudy's father was quoted after the arrest as saying: 'They found a first black man, then they had to let him go, so now they've grabbed another one.'[7] Rudy had been extradited back to Italy by early December and those who believe Amanda and Raffaele to be innocent assert that Mignini simply had no choice but to save face. If his theory that this crime was perpetrated by three individuals was to hold water, he would simply have to swap one black man for another and carry on.

At this point it might be more pertinent to go back and ask what on earth compelled Amanda to point the finger at Patrick in the first instance? And in the same vein, why did Raffaele suddenly change his story and retract Amanda's alibi? Where they two entirely separate events, or did one trigger the other?

There's no doubt that the turning point in the investigation was the evening on which Raffaele and Amanda changed their original stories and effectively cancelled out each other's alibi. On 5 November Raffaele told police that, contrary to what he had previously said, Amanda had not been with him on the night of 1 November; he now recalled that they had parted company at 9.00pm, with Amanda returning to his flat at around 1.00am. On the same evening, in a separate interview room, Amanda told investigators that she had met up with Patrick on the night of the murder and that they had travelled together to the cottage where she 'remembered confusedly that he killed her'.[8]

Although investigators already had their suspicions before this turn of events, it's fair to say that it was at this point that the case headed in a different direction; the couple's mutual alibi was gone, and Amanda had placed herself at the crime scene. It is no surprise that what followed was Amanda, Raffaele and Patrick's very public arrest. But was this piece of evidence a knee-jerk reaction on the part of Amanda after hearing that her boyfriend had effectively thrown her under a bus and, realising that the game was up, searched around for the nearest black scapegoat? Or was it a coerced confession drawn out on the back of hours of torturous interrogation in a language which was not her first, dragged out of her through sheer desperation for it all to stop?

Perhaps most important is to ask first, what made Raffaele change his story and retract Amanda's alibi, allegedly triggering her accusation of an innocent Patrick? The explanation that Raffaele allegedly gave at the time was: 'I told you a lot of bullshit in my earlier statement, because she'd convinced me that her version of what happened was right, and I didn't think of the inconsistencies.'[9] On the face of it, this is damaging to Amanda to say the least. It strengthens the narrative that Amanda had a magical, sexual hold over the other accused men, and that Raffaele had been coerced by her into giving her an alibi which he then rightfully retracted.

In his book, Raffaele denies this, explaining simply that 'one day blended into another in my mind', and that during his interrogation he had simply mixed-up Halloween with the 1 November and recounted the details from the wrong night. He says that he asked officers if November 1 was a Tuesday or a Thursday (knowing that Amanda worked at Le Chic on a Thursday) but wasn't allowed access to a calendar for reference to help him remember. Subsequently, what the police ended up with was a 'mash up of the events of 31 October and 1 November, most of which, I have to admit, was the result of my own confusion'.[10] Of his comment about Amanda, he says that he objected to the paragraph about her lies when signing his statement that evening, and even asked for it to be changed, implying that his words were, if not made up, then certainly misconstrued. Police assured him that he needn't worry about it, and it was included in its original form in his final statement.

One of the main problems for most people who think that Amanda had something to do with the murder is her inability to tell the truth. They allege that she lied. They allege that she willingly threw an innocent man to the wolves to save herself. She lied, she lied, she lied. She is accused of lying at every step of the investigation, but the lie which angers people the most appears to be her accusation of Patrick. It was not coerced, they say, it wasn't a mistake, it was a plain old-fashioned lie, created to deflect the heat from her. With the benefit of hindsight, we now know that Patrick could not have had anything to do with the murder of Meredith. He had a cast-iron alibi and was nowhere near the cottage on that evening. Knowing this brings even more focus onto Amanda's accusation, because whether or not she was in the cottage that night, Patrick most certainly wasn't.

So why did she do it? Firstly, there exists the theory that she knew full well that Rudy had been in the cottage that night, because she had been there with him, carrying out a murder. Therefore, she named Patrick, a black man, in an attempt to cover for her black co-conspirator in the hope that he would repay the favour and keep quiet about her involvement. In this instance her reasoning for accusing Patrick appears to be racially motivated and further points to her guilt. She was, they say, afraid that Rudy may have been seen entering or leaving the cottage, and therefore pointed the police in the direction of an alternative black man, neatly diverting attention away from Rudy.

Rudy himself, understandably, backs the racial theory via a television interview he gave in 2016, although clearly not the element whereby Amanda was covering for him, because of course he must support the narrative that while he was at the scene of the crime, he had absolutely nothing to do with the actual murder. He claims that '(1) her co-murderer, Sollecito, told her a person of colour had been in the house with them and (2) that she had received a text from Lumumba earlier that evening.'[11] She had therefore panicked and blamed the only other black man she knew. Rudy.

The counter theory by those who believe Amanda to be innocent is that her accusation against Patrick was entirely coerced. She asserts that she was repeatedly hit around the head during the interrogation and told to remember the facts correctly. She was tricked into talking to officers without an interpreter present, with no legal representation and no recording taking place. When the interpreter did arrive at around 12.30am she says that 'it's inconceivable to me now that all the questioning up to that point had been in Italian'.[12]

Describing the moment that she gave them Patrick's name as a culmination of the pressure, she says that in that moment she:

> truly thought that I remembered having met somebody. I didn't understand what was happening to me. I didn't understand that I was about to implicate the wrong person. I didn't understand what was at stake. I didn't think I was making it up. My mind put together incoherent images. The image that came to me was Patrick's face.[13]

So, those who believe Amanda to be innocent describe the result of what happened to her as a classic false confession; something which has gained more credibility in recent years following the documentary *Making a Murderer* which aired on Netflix in 2015. There are now several documentaries on Netflix alone based around the phenomena of false confessions and how they can be, and have been, coerced, but back in 2007 it was a virtually alien concept; it would have been almost impossible to imagine a scenario in which someone would willingly implicate themselves or someone else in a criminal act in which they had no involvement. Interestingly, in the earlier versions of the documentaries made about this case from around 2008–11, coercion is barely mentioned. It's only in more recent years that this issue is addressed; beforehand she is simply described as having changed her story.

So, what is a coerced confession? Essentially, it is a confession which is given as the result of coercive police interrogation techniques which can include confusing the defendant, lying to them about evidence, threatening them with lengthy prison sentences or other punishment, and physically and/or mentally exhausting them. And this is exactly what Amanda described happening to her in the interrogation room. The problem is, of course, the interrogation was never recorded so this whole issue will always remain a case of her word against the police. The courts, ultimately, did not believe her.

And nor do many, many others, whose outlook is incredibly sceptical and see this as at best an attempt to get herself released, and at worst a deliberate act of vindictiveness, possibly racially motivated, against an innocent man. It further perpetuates her detractors' view of Amanda as a manipulative liar and a slanderer as opposed to an innocent young woman, terrified in a country where she is being interrogated in a language which is not her first.

Heading for Trial

The police now held Amanda, Raffaele and Rudy safely in custody, and meanwhile the forensic work continued. Alongside the evidence which placed Rudy at the scene and led to his arrest, investigators had also found a size nine footprint in blood on a pillowcase at the crime scene, which they believed belonged to Raffaele. In mid-November, Patrizia Stefanoni found traces of Amanda's DNA on the handle of the knife which had been taken from Raffaele's apartment, and traces of Meredith's DNA on the blade. The forensic case was now building against all three suspects.

At this point the police had firmly placed Rudy Guede at the scene of the murder through his handprint, DNA from the vaginal swab and the toilet paper from the unflushed toilet, along with his blood mixed with Meredith's. They had also at this stage placed Amanda and Raffaele at the scene, albeit with weaker evidence; Amanda and Meredith's DNA on the knife they suspected to be the murder weapon, alongside the size nine footprint. The knife, of course, had been found at Raffaele's allegedly bleach-smelling apartment. In what appeared to be a positive break for him, however, it wasn't long after this that the size nine footprint was confirmed to be consistent with Rudy's Nike Outbreak 2 shoes, rather than Raffaele's Nike Airforce 1.

By 28 November the forensic police in Rome reported back fully on the test results of the evidence they had gathered in the cottage immediately following the murder, which included mixed traces of blood from Amanda and Meredith on the bidet, basin and cotton bud box in the bathroom. Unfortunately for Raffaele, while the other footprint seemed not to implicate him, they now concluded that the bloody footprint on the bathmat was consistent with the size of his foot.

On 18 December, forty-seven days after the murder, a fresh survey of the cottage was carried out, attended by Mignini and Stefanoni, whereupon more forensic evidence, which would again prove to be incredibly contentious, was found. Amanda's lawyer, Luciano Ghirga, and Raffaele's lawyer, Luca Maori, were witness to this and noted that the crime scene was a mess, with the mattress having been moved and the bloody cushion stuffed into a cupboard among other things, beginning to cause them concern that the scene had been compromised.

During this search, which was recorded on video tape and later used in evidence during the trials, one of the officers found the missing bra clasp under a rug near the desk in Meredith's room, about a metre or so away from where it had first been found back on 2 November and pointed out to the forensic team by Luca Lalli.

It was also during this visit that the team decided to test various areas of the cottage using Luminol, a substance used by investigators to create a light-producing chemical reaction should it come into contact with certain substances including, but not limited to, haemoglobin, a protein found in blood. Clearly, blood tends to be the specific target when Luminol is used in a criminal investigation, particularly useful as samples which are not visible to the naked eye (for example because they have been removed in an attempt to clean up) will become visible once the chemical reaction takes place.

This particular spray revealed various footprints around the cottage, which investigators believed to have been made in blood. Due to their measurements, they suggested that they proved 'probable identity' of Amanda and Raffaele. Amanda's were pointing towards the door from within her bedroom, and in the corridor, pointing towards Meredith's door. A small footprint was found on a cushion under Meredith's body and again proved 'probable identity' of Amanda. Luminol also picked up traces of what was thought to be blood in Filomena's room; one sample belonged to Meredith and one to Meredith and Amanda mixed together.

Back at her office, Stefanoni found traces of Raffaele and Meredith's DNA on the bra clasp, and traces of Rudy's DNA on the bra strap. The police now felt that they had forensically placed all three of the suspects at the scene, albeit some more strongly than others. Rudy's presence had already been established, and now they had placed their other suspects there by virtue of footprints in blood, mixed blood with the victim and DNA on the cut bra clasp. Bingo.

It wasn't just DNA evidence that drove the investigation forward over the following months though. In the ten months between January and November 2008 several key issues came to light, not least the discovery of some apparent eyewitnesses from the night of, and following, the murder.

First, in January 2008, Hekuran Kokomani came forward to the police and gave a statement to the effect that he had witnessed a male and a female in the road outside the cottage at No. 7, Via della Pergola, on either the evening of Halloween or 1 November. When he attempted to drive past, the female threatened him with the knife, cautioning him in Italian that he should 'get out of here or I'll show you!' When Kokomani reacted to her the male, he says, told him to 'forget it, she's a girl, she can't do anything to you'.[1] He drove on, then encountered a black male standing in front of the cottage, at which point he then says that the female had admonished all three of them not to show their faces. He would later identify them as Rudy, Raffaele and Amanda. He had, he said, not come forward before as he was scared of getting involved.

Local journalist Antioco Fois had previously, and rather successfully, been conducting his own investigations following the murder. He was in fact the person who had tracked down Nara Capezzali back in November and broken her story of screams and footsteps to the public, also passing on the information to the investigators at the time, much to their chagrin. In January 2008 he uncovered a further witness, local homeless man Antonio Curatolo, who revealed that he had seen Amanda and Raffaele 'hugging and kissing'[2] between 11.00pm and midnight on the night of the murder. He described their manner as agitated and that he had the impression that they were checking on something; he claimed to have seen them sitting on a low wall in the basketball court near the cottage. Curatolo was, he said, scared to get involved but Fois eventually persuaded him to talk to Mignini, and almost a month later he gave his official statement to the prosecutor. He had, he said, been questioned by the *Carabinieri* the day after the murder but as he had not recognised the couple until he saw their faces in the paper later on, had not felt the need to say anything at that stage.

Fois would come up trumps again, but not for another ten months when he introduced local grocer, Marco Quintavalle, to Mignini in November 2008. He had confided in Fois that early in the morning of 2 November 2007, just over a year ago at the time of telling, he had witnessed Amanda in his supermarket at the time when she claimed to have been asleep in Raffaele's flat. She was, he said, looking as though she was 'trying to hide'.[3] He was sure of her identity, having remembered her accompanying regular customer Raffaele a couple of weeks before the murder, the sighting being noteworthy enough for him to register and remember her. Although he couldn't confirm whether or not she actually bought anything on the morning of 2 November, he was sure that she had headed down to the aisle where cleaning products and bleach were kept. It's still slightly unclear as to why he didn't mention this at the time as, like Curatolo, he had been shown photographs of Amanda and Raffaele by police following the murder and although he recognised them, he had said nothing about Amanda's alleged presence in his shop. He told Fois that he hadn't come forward at that point because first, he was not 100 per cent sure it was Amanda, given that she had been wearing a scarf and hat. Second, and more probable, he, like many of the others, simply did not want to get involved.

Although not quite as dramatic as a last-minute witness, but certainly more potentially damaging, the prosecution would have been delighted when, on 26 March 2008, Rudy changed his story yet again and now claimed that Amanda was in fact responsible for Meredith's murder. He now described a scenario in which he and Meredith started to kiss when he suddenly needed to go to the toilet and left her alone. He says he heard the doorbell ring and Meredith call out 'who is it?' Then he heard her say tensely 'we need to talk', to which a voice that he thought was Amanda's replied, 'what's happening?' As he was by now listening to his iPod, he heard none of the remaining conversation until he was interrupted by a loud scream. Rushing out of the bathroom he witnessed a man standing with his back to him who then threatened him with a knife, shouting to an unseen accomplice: 'He's black. I've found a black guy; I've found the culprit. Let's go.'[4] Rudy then attempted to help Meredith by fetching towels to try and staunch the blood, before fleeing the scene. Although he says he did not see Amanda directly, he is sure that he could identify her by the silhouette he claims to have fleetingly seen.

It wasn't until 19 April 2008 that the pathologists presented their report to analyse exactly how Meredith had died. The conclusions were that she had engaged in sexual activity, but it was not clear whether it was consensual or not. The cause of death was asphyxiation caused by strangling and internal bleeding. They now put her time of death between 8.45pm on 1 November and 12.50am on 2 November.

Things were now moving fairly fast, by Italy's standards. By 28 May Mignini had brought in fellow prosecutor Manuela Comodi to help him present the case, and on 19 June they signed a decree formally notifying Amanda and Raffaele that their investigation was complete. In July, Mignini formally requested that they stand trial under the accusation that the three had forced a sex game on an unwilling Meredith and had killed her when she refused. They had then stolen the 300 euros which had gone missing from Meredith's room along with her two mobile phones, and Amanda and Raffaele had then staged a break-in. He also wanted them both charged with carrying a weapon, as his theory held that the knife found in Raffaele's apartment and believed to be the murder weapon, had been carried by one or other of them from his apartment to Amanda's cottage in order to carry out the murder. Lastly, he asked that Amanda be tried for *calunnia* (slander) against Patrick Lumumba.

Following a series of hearings, on the 15 September 2008 it was confirmed that Rudy's lawyers' request that he be tried separately to Amanda and Raffaele in a fast-track trial, was accepted by Judge Paolo Micheli. It was agreed that on the day of his trial the decision would be made as to whether or not Amanda and Raffaele's case should also go to a separate trial. And so it was that on 28 October 2008, almost a year to the day since Meredith was murdered, Rudy's fast track trial took place. He was found guilty of murder, following twelve hours of deliberation by Judge Micheli. He was sentenced to thirty years in jail.

Micheli came to his conclusion based on the proposals put to the court by prosecutors Mignini and his co-prosecutor Manuela Comodi, who had been tasked with dealing mainly with the forensic evidence. Their reconstruction of the crime went like this:

Rudy, Amanda and Raffaele were all in a drugged state on the day of the murder. Amanda and Meredith were at the cottage together when Amanda then let Raffaele and Rudy into the house. Meredith was tired, and angry at Amanda's promiscuous behaviour, sparking a huge row. Rudy, who was attracted to Amanda, would be willing to do anything she asked; Mignini asserts that Amanda asked him to 'soften up' Meredith in order for them all to take part in an erotic game.

Meredith refused to take part, whereupon the other three became infuriated with her. They attempted to strangle her and threatened her with knives. Rudy tried to rape her. The two men held Meredith by the arms while Amanda taunted her with the knife and, eventually, she 'plunged the blade into Meredith's neck.' All three of them were involved in ripping her bra from her body, and then dragged Meredith's body from where the murder had taken place in front of her wardrobe to the middle of the floor where they placed the quilt over her body. This last act, Mignini asserted, confirmed that 'the killer and victim were acquaintances or friends, and the killer was not a habitual murderer'. They then fled the scene, stealing 300 euros before they left; Rudy headed home but the two lovers returned to the cottage to destroy vital evidence and stage a burglary, during which they were surprised by the unexpected arrival of the *Polizia Postale* on the morning of the 2 November.

Judge Micheli agreed that the evidence proved that several attackers had been involved in the crime and so, on the same day as finding Rudy guilty, he confirmed that Amanda and Raffaele would indeed be required to stand trial for murder with a date set for January the following year. Amanda would also be on trial concurrently for the slander of Patrick Lumumba.

TRIAL

George Clooney's wife

R udy, a convicted murderer. Amanda and Raffaele, innocent until proven guilty. And yet, the sparse media coverage of Rudy's trial would pale into insignificance in the face of what was to come. It's hard to argue that all three of the suspects were not equally involved in this case, whether through guilt or by association. So why is it that Amanda remains the main focus of interest whereas Rudy, the convicted killer, is largely forgotten? And why, of the two young adults about to face trial, does the focus remain firmly on Amanda and not her co-defendant Raffaele?

Rudy, the little man

No matter what the differing opinions on this case, the fact remains that Rudy Guede is the only suspect who was ultimately found guilty and served a sentence, albeit a reduced one, for the crime of murdering Meredith Kercher. And yet, it seems that he is the one character whose story remains the most elusive. Perhaps this is in part because his trial, compared to those of Amanda and Raffaele, was relatively simple. Fast track, reduced sentence, release. If it was reported in the papers at the time, it certainly did not attract a fraction of the attention that Amanda and Raffaele's trials would muster. He has participated in some interviews since his conviction, but in comparison to the other defendants, this lack of reference leads to a fair amount of confusion about Rudy. In particular the details about his early life are, while there for the discovery, less accessible and more confusing than the others, with seemingly the most trustworthy sources being his family and friends from childhood. Most of these sources were interviewed by the police in the course of their investigations, including Giacomo Benedetti, who was instrumental in helping the police to track down Rudy back in November 2007, and Rudy's father, Roger, who was located by police while the search for Rudy was on. The facts are there to be found, but the question is, could anyone really be bothered to find them?

Rudy Guede was born in Ivory Coast on 26 December 1986, and although accounts can be contradictory, most seem to agree that Rudy had an unhappy childhood. His home life was certainly anything but stable; Roger, his father, says Rudy was abandoned by his mother, Agnes when he was only a few days old and was then moved from one foster home to another. In this narrative, however, Roger does not make it clear exactly what parental role he was playing at this point. Some accounts talk of Roger and Agnes divorcing when Rudy was 10, although it's even not clear whether they were ever actually married; other sources explain that Roger practiced polygamy and had several girlfriends, or wives, on the go at any one time and that Agnes was one of many of Roger's girlfriends. In fact, one of the others was concurrently pregnant, meaning that Rudy has a half-brother almost exactly the same age as him living in Ivory Coast. Roger's version that Rudy's mother abandoned him might be taken with a pinch of salt; other more objective reports say that Agnes moved in with Roger's sister, Georgette, when Rudy was tiny, who then took over his care and moved from town to town within Ivory Coast, this transient lifestyle meaning that a young Rudy could never truly make friends.

Roger went to seek work in Italy and fetched Rudy to the country with him when he was 5 years old, followed by his Aunt Georgette. Rudy and his father became distant, with Rudy very occasionally returning to visit his mother, following which at a later date he decided that he had no desire to go back to Ivory Coast again. In contrast, Roger felt the pull to return, and did so, he says, when Rudy was around 15, with every intention of coming back to fetch him. This intention was scuppered by, among other things, a lost passport and the outbreak of civil war, so Rudy was left behind in Italy with Roger's girlfriend, with whom Rudy did not get along at all. It was at this point, or soon after, that social services stepped in and placed Rudy with a wealthy foster family. On his father's subsequent visits to Italy, Rudy apparently wanted nothing to do with him and their relationship dwindled even further.

It's perhaps understandable that Roger might like to paint himself in a slightly better light by the suggestion that it was Agnes who had abandoned Rudy at just a few days old. More likely, it seems, is that Agnes leant heavily on his sister Georgette for support, who gradually took over Rudy's full-time care from a struggling Agnes before she and Roger took him to Italy when he was 5, garnering little complaint from Agnes.

Rudy, however, tells a different story. At the time of writing, he had just published a book called *The Benefit of the Doubt*, which sank almost immediately into oblivion and was only available in Italy, but which purported to confirm his version of the events of that night alongside more details of his childhood, but in the absence of any information back then, detectives did discover during their investigations a blog of his in which he reportedly describes an autobiographical account titled *A house without a roof is like a child without a father*. Written in the third person, it describes a child who has been raised by an aunt and in doing so, has been robbed of his mother and father. He describes an emotional reunion with his mother, after which they become inseparable but, heartbreakingly, there follows a day when she went away for good 'and didn't even say goodbye'.[1]

Rudy elaborates more about his childhood, and indeed his conviction, during a televised interview with journalist Franca Leosini on an Italian show called *Storie Maledette* (*Cursed Stories*) aired in 2016. He paints a slightly different picture of the first few years of his life, explaining that he was very happy living with his mother in Ivory Coast until he was 5 years old, when his aunt suddenly appeared out of the blue and whisked him away to Italy to live with his father, a complete stranger to him. He even describes a physical tussle between his mother and his aunt, with himself stuck in the middle. He relates that his father conjured up a constant stream of girlfriends, and that although he had a fairly good relationship with him, he always felt that he was a burden, not quite included. Roger often worked away, and by the time Rudy was 7 years old he would often come home from school to an empty house and be forced to fend for himself; a self-reliant, independent child – 'I was sort of a little man', he says.[2]

By all accounts, while growing up Rudy did have some good luck with some of the adult influences in his life; first would be meeting a teacher named Ivana Tiberi who witnessed his neglectful lifestyle and took him under her wing. During his interview he describes his saviour who became his 'surrogate mother figure', and Leosini talks of the bond between them which she suggests to Rudy would become 'endurable and unbreakable'.[3]

Another opportunity came his way in the form of the wealthy Caporali family. Rudy explains that due to Roger's constant absence, he was placed with the family as a foster child; his new father happened to be a basketball sponsor, a sport Rudy loved and was apparently talented enough to have pursued a career in had he been tall enough. He holidayed in the sun, he skied. He had seemingly been plucked from neglect into an idyllic home and Leosini asks him: was this your fairy-tale ending?

It seems that the answer was no. He was still unsettled and dropped out of various courses and jobs organised for him by the Caporalis. He was a truant and, by his own admission, 'caused them anger'[4] with his errant behaviour; when he turned 18 and was no longer eligible to be fostered, he went back to live with his aunt. The Caporalis gave him a job as a gardener in their villa just outside Perugia, but as was becoming a regular occurrence he proved to be unreliable, and they were no longer able to trust him. According to an interview with Paolo Caporali, after Rudy's arrest they had had no contact at all for the year prior to the murder.

His route to Perugia in 2007 was apparently via his aunt Georgette, with whom he returned to live after leaving the Caporalis, during which time she helped him get a job in a café; he was now living in Milan with a girlfriend, and all seemed to be going well for him. However, he abruptly lost his job for reasons which remain unclear, and he had drifted back to Perugia by the late spring of 2007.

It's not only his childhood that Rudy perhaps puts a positive spin on but also, understandably, his reputation as a drug- and alcohol-addicted drifter and crook, who was described during Amanda and Raffaele's appeal by their lawyers as skilful in breaking and entering. Rudy claims that he only occasionally drank, and other than the odd joint he never touched drugs; Leosini puts to him in the interview that 'close friends swear they never saw you drunk'.[5] He is adamant that he is not a petty crook.

One story which is often retold about him, perhaps due to the fact that it happened just a week before the murder, is that during the investigation detectives learned from the *Carabinieri* in Milan that Rudy had been accused of attempted robbery after they discovered him in a kindergarten at night carrying a rucksack containing a large kitchen knife, a hammer, and a laptop and mobile phone, allegedly stolen from a lawyers' office in Perugia a week or so previously.

Rudy tells a very different version during his interview with Leosini. First, he claims that the laptop he was carrying was his own, bought a few days earlier from a flea market. On the night in question, he'd been out with friends, but at some point during the evening he lost them and happened to bump into a stranger who offered him a place to stay – the local kindergarten. This person's wife happened to work there, so of course he had a set of keys and was happy to let Rudy in to sleep for the night. When he was discovered in the morning by the owner, she called the police who took him in and discovered that the laptop he was carrying was stolen, unbeknownst to Rudy of course, who had innocently purchased it the week before. He explains that the police 'took this event out of proportion', and 'manipulated the facts to make me look like a professional thief'. He explained away the knife in his possession – it had simply been lying on the owner's desk and he had no idea how it found its way into his bag. He claims that this was backed up by the owner, who 'told them they'd made a mistake'[6] regarding the knife. Rudy's reputation as a thief is, he says, incorrect and that the only time he had ever been arrested in his life was following this 'misunderstanding' at the kindergarten.

Rudy's version is far-fetched to say the least, but whatever the events of that evening, Rudy's lifestyle was certainly unconventional and by the time of Meredith's murder he apparently had gained a bit of a reputation in Perugia. He would drink too much, dance on the tables, and people – particularly female – didn't like to dance too close to Rudy, 'because when he got sweaty, he stank'.[7]

Since his arrest and conviction, Rudy, or those who stand behind him, have worked to create a different image of him to that of a knife-wielding murderer. During his interview with Leosini, he presents himself very well, he's well-dressed, articulate and almost unbelievably humble. Whether or not this whole persona is a fabrication, it does seem that by most accounts, or certainly those which have come to light, those who knew him in childhood hold overwhelming memories of him as quiet, sweet, shy and on the surface, seemingly incapable of hurting a fly.

As always, interpretation is everything. Rudy's interview with Leosini is uncomfortable to watch, with the older female host at times almost openly flirting with him, teasing him about his apparent coyness at recalling his alleged kiss with Meredith, and at one point – in a conversation which is at best inappropriate and at worst offensive – implores him to tell her about the moment he met 'the beautiful Meredith', for she has, of course, been tragically forgotten in all of this, but perhaps Rudy can remedy that by painting her, and the viewers, a picture of the victim. Interestingly, the word murder is rarely, if ever, used, with the night described as the 'tragedy', or the 'sad event'.[8] By the end of the interview Rudy has risen to almost saint-like status, with soft focus footage showing him reading, painting, wandering around the garden to the backdrop of romantic music.

Raffaele, a handsome boy of quiet intelligence

On the face of it, Raffaele Sollecito and Rudy Guede could not have been more different characters than if they had been created as a plot device in a film. One came from a broken background and was all but abandoned by his father at a young age, and the other lived a wealthy, sheltered life until leaving home to study at university and even then, had the full emotional, and particularly financial, support of this family. In actual fact though, there may be more similarities between the two than at first appears.

Raffaele himself doesn't tell us much at all about his childhood in his book, but rather the details are pieced together from other sources – albeit some through direct interviews with him by other authors. Born on 26 March 1984 in Giovinazzo, a small town near Bari in southern Italy, his childhood certainly started out happily enough; but in a parallel with Rudy, he did also suffer from his parents parting ways when he was 8 years old. Up until then, his mother's world had revolved around looking after Raffaele and his sister Vanessa, who was six years older than him, having given up a

21-year-old Meredith Kercher, a bright, popular student whose life was full of laughter. This image of her was used by the police and distributed to the press and would become synonymous with her murder on 1 November 2007. British News Service / Alamy Stock Photo

Meredith's family: mother Arline (left), father John and sister Stephanie arrive in Italy following her death and attend a press conference on 6 November 2007. Trinity Mirror / Mirrorpix / Alamy Stock Photo

The historical centre of Perugia, capital of the Umbrian region of Italy. Adobe Stock

No. 7, Via della Pergola, the cottage shared by Meredith Kercher, Amanda Knox, Filomena Romanelli and Laura Mezzetti. Taken on 21 January 2008; the police tape can still be seen cordoning off the front door. Filomena's bedroom window is situated to the left of the brick pillar. REUTERS / Alamy Stock Photo

Amanda is questioned by police outside the murder scene when they return to the cottage on 5 November 2007, just before her subsequent arrest. Trinity Mirror / Mirrorpix / Alamy Stock Photo

Amanda and Raffaele arrive at a court hearing accompanied by police on 26 September 2008 just a month before Rudy's fast-track trial takes place. REUTERS / Alamy Stock Photo

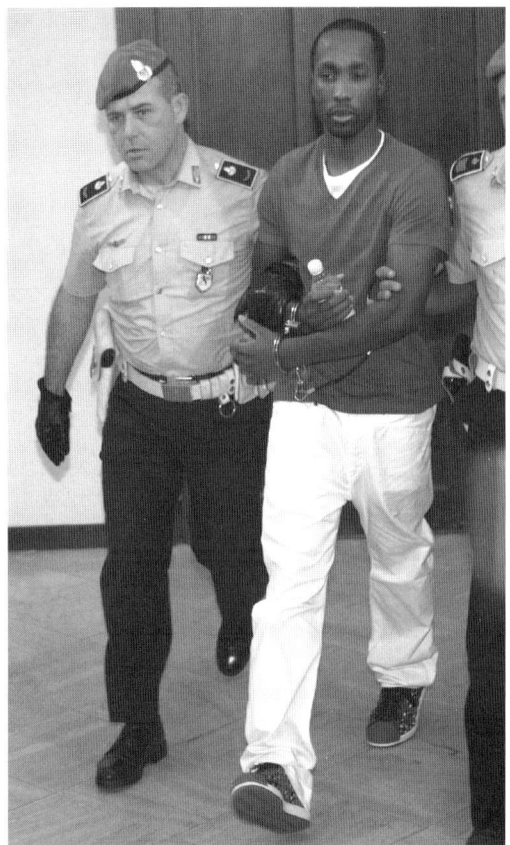

Rudy heads back to a court hearing to determine his fast-track trial accompanied by police on 16 September 2008. REUTERS / Alamy Stock Photo

Rudy giving a thumbs up sign to an unknown person, back in court in November 2008 to appeal his sentence, which would be reduced to sixteen years in December 2008. REUTERS / Alamy Stock Photo

Public minister Giuliano Mignini arrives at court 14 January 2009 ahead of Amanda and Raffaele's first trial. LaPresse / Alamy Stock Photo

Patrick Lumumba leaving court having attended a session of Amanda and Raffaele's retrial in Florence, January 2014. REUTERS / Alamy Stock Photo

Raffaele greets one of his lawyers, Giulia Buongiorno, during one of his appeal sessions on 30 September 2011 ahead of the successful result in October 2011. REUTERS / Alamy Stock Photo

Amanda gives evidence to the court at their first trial during the second day of her testimony on 13 June 2009. REUTERS / Alamy Stock Photo

Members of the court visit the crime scene on 18 April 2009 during the first trial and can be seen assessing the window where the alleged break-in took place. REUTERS / Alamy Stock Photo

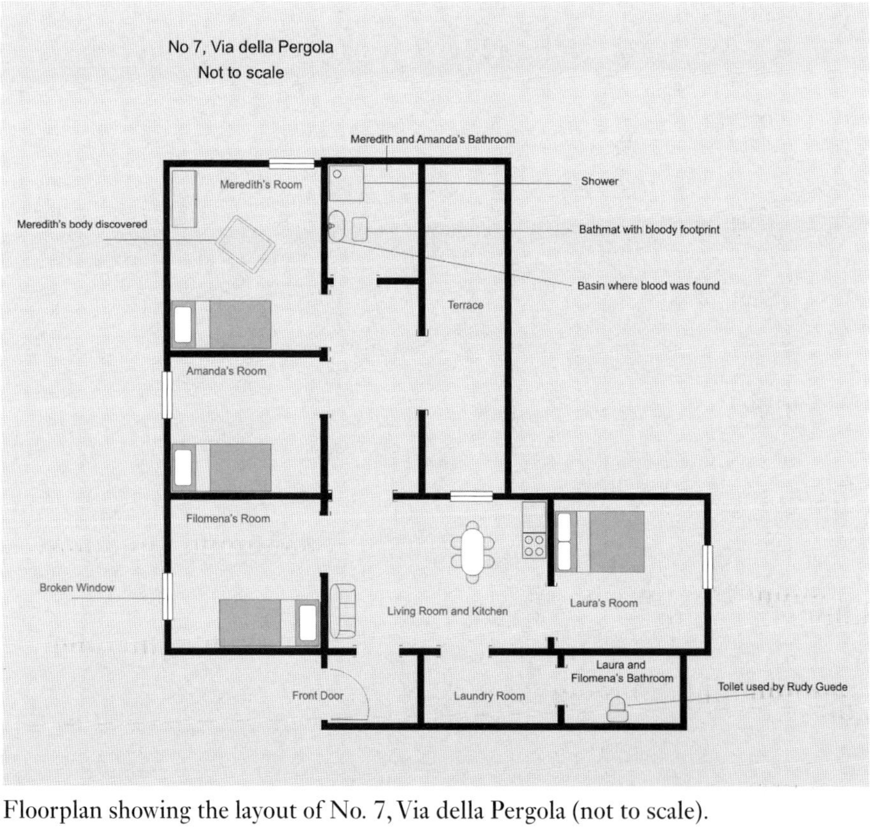

Floorplan showing the layout of No. 7, Via della Pergola (not to scale).

Celine Buckens plays Talitha Campbell in the dock on trial for murder in *Showtrial*, 2021. Her character is speculated to be loosely based on Amanda Knox. Album / Alamy Stock Photo

Actors Matt Damon and Abigail Breslin talk to director Tom McCarthy on the set of *Stillwater* released in 2021 which was reported to be 'directly inspired by the Amanda Knox saga'. Entertainment Pictures / Alamy Stock Photo

Amanda Knox with husband Christopher Robinson in New York on 29 September 2016. They co-host the podcast *Labyrinths* under their company *Knox Robinson Productions* and have also co-written an anthology of poems. Everett Collection Inc / Alamy Stock Photo

Raffaele Sollecito appears on television show *Otto e Mezzo* on 6 October 2015 to promote his new book *Step out of the night: Everything you never imagined about me* (translation from Italian title *Un passo fuori dalla notte: Tutto quello che non avete mai immaginato di me*) in which he talks about the detrimental effect the case had on his life, then and now. WENN Rights Ltd / Alamy Stock Photo successful accountancy career to do so. Raffaele describes himself as the centre of this attention, and that although both of his parents were devoted to him, it was he who was the particular apple of his mother's eye. By his own admission, as a result of this he grew up in a 'softened' environment, protected from harm. He describes himself as 'very discreet, calm and introverted',[9] and he explains that his shyness came about in a bid to avoid saying the wrong thing and looking stupid or becoming a nuisance, perhaps following the confusion of the separation of his parents.

The divorce hit his mother hard; Francesco, Raffaele's father, had been her only true love and while she remained single following the split, he moved on fairly swiftly to a life with his new wife, Mara. Despite the separation, both parents still continued to pour love on Raffaele, something which he would later go on to describe as 'fussing', and which drove him to choose Perugia as his place of study in order to put some physical distance between them. Contrary to this though, he is also reported as finding it difficult to settle due to a combination of shyness and homesickness.

He had spent the first two years in Perugia in the ONAOSI, a kind of halls of residence reserved for the orphaned children of doctors, but also available to the children of living doctors and this is how he found himself in what might be described as luxurious accommodation which did, nonetheless, have an air of the boarding school surrounding it. He took time out on an Erasmus in Germany, following which he returned to Perugia in 2006; not to the ONAOSI, but now living in private residence, a flat or apartment known as a *monolocale*. It was nestled in a medieval building on Corps Garibaldi and came with the luxury of maid service, paid for by his wealthy father. By October 2007 he was due to graduate at the age of 23.

That Amanda and Raffaele smoked pot together comes up on numerous occasions, and indeed Amanda smoking with her female flatmates and the boys downstairs. They are quite open about it and in his book, he admits to experimenting with various drugs in his late teens, including ecstasy, poppers, and just once, cocaine. Pot was his drug of choice though; he describes his use as an occasional habit. Some of the more tabloid versions of events describe him as a 'mummy's boy', 'lazy', and that on the first day of university he 'rolled up in Perugia late, stoned and disorganised'.[10]

So, at this point certain parallels could be drawn between Rudy Guede and Raffaele Sollecito. They were both children of separated parents who enjoyed, if not a serious habit, then certainly recreational drug use. Technically they both shared the privilege of money and decent schooling, even if Rudy's had been offered to him later in life by foster parents, and even if he hadn't quite made the most of it as Raffaele had. One could even go so far as to draw similarities in their personalities as, depending on the source, childhood friends described them both with the same nostalgic reminiscence, describing kind, quiet, shy boys.

Although Raffaele's book itself doesn't tell us much at all about his childhood in his own words, it does of course paint the overall persona which he would like to portray, that of the kind, shy boy his friends remember. Other sources make much of the darker side of his personality, whether or not they are based in fact. From childhood he had become interested in knives, using them to carve inscriptions into trees and made a habit of carrying them around with him most of the time. Friends say they became almost part of his persona, although he was always very respectful of them, unwilling to allow anyone to get hurt by using them recklessly; naturally, this childhood link to a potential murder weapon could not be ignored by the press. He was into Japanese manga which can, at times, be pornographic and violent in its content, and one particular issue reported from his college years was getting into trouble with authorities who had caught him watching violent pornography which included images of bestiality. Raffaele's version of this episode was that he, along with some friends, watched a DVD together for a laugh, having heard that they would witness some sort of sexual activity involving a pig, but were all disappointed in the low-quality offering.

Even now, Raffaele is relegated to the role of Amanda Knox's ex-boyfriend in a spin on the general trend of successful women continually being described in the press as the 'wife of' some celebrity or other, the most obvious example being that of Amal Clooney, a successful barrister, identified consistently in the media as simply 'George Clooney's wife'. In the case of Amanda and Raffaele though, sex sells, and so the attractive, female Amanda takes centre stage. At the time of writing, Raffaele is engaged to be married; the headline in the *Daily Mail* at the time read: *Amanda Knox's ex-fiancé Raffaele Sollecito announces he is engaged again to his new girlfriend.*[11] Similarly, a piece written in May 2022 entitled *What Happened to Amanda Knox's Ex-Boyfriend, Raffaele Sollecito?*[12] spends approximately 15 per cent of the article answering that question, and the rest discussing Amanda Knox and the 'shady moments' which occurred during the investigation into Meredith's murder. It seems that nobody really cares at all what happened to Raffaele.

Raffaele's character in the media seems to have settled as a hybrid of a virginal, timid pothead and a knife-obsessed, hardcore porn addict. Much is made of the contents of a blog he wrote around the time of the year he spent in Germany in which he wrote that he 'wanted to find bigger thrills which will surprise me'.[13] Translation is key here; by some accounts what he actually wrote was that he would hope to find 'stronger emotions'.[14] Raffaele himself, still a virgin at this point, says that he was simply talking about sex.

Amanda, Foxy Knoxy

In contrast to Raffaele, Amanda's book contains an awful lot more information about her childhood and upbringing, perhaps because she has more at stake and a much worse reputation in the media which she is attempting to quell. While Rudy and Raffaele seem generally to be viewed as male puppets simply doing as they are told, the public view of Amanda broadly splits into two camps; in basic terms she's viewed as either quirky yet innocent, or a psychopath. Her behaviour undeniably drew unwanted attention to her during the investigation, and broadly speaking this behaviour is explained in favourable reports as down to a loveable quirkiness, in less favourable as bordering on narcissistic.

The picture that Amanda and her supporters paint is that of an intelligent, independent young woman, keen to view the world on her own terms with as little help as possible. Amanda is someone who admits to her mistakes, who is goofy, socially awkward and who sometimes misreads the room and comes out with totally the wrong, embarrassing statement. She doesn't share the shame though; if others think it's weird that she might start singing in front of them unprovoked in the middle of a restaurant, that's their problem, not hers. She was young, courageous, finding her own maturity. She's a misfit, a geek, clumsy with words, blunt and to the point. She's simply being herself. The opinion which Meredith's friends apparently had of her was that she was annoying, promiscuous, thoughtless, selfish, messy and weird. Where she would say quirky, others would say irritating.

Among Amanda's other perceived traits are that she's fun loving, enjoys a drink, enjoys a joint, enjoys sex. And this is where her issues arise or, more accurately, where the public appears to have an issue with her. Probably the most famous description of Amanda is that of her nickname: 'Foxy Knoxy', which became public when, following the murder, the press did some pretty thorough investigating into her background and unearthed her nickname from school. Never mind that this nickname was given to her due to her wily skills as a soccer player; it fitted in perfectly with the image of a sex-crazed killer and so it stuck, and the world's perception of Amanda was consolidated.

Despite all of this, what really sets Amanda apart from her two co-defendants is her sex life, and the public's fascination with it. On 22 November 2007, Amanda was told that she was HIV positive. She was incarcerated at the time and wrote in her prison diary the names of the seven men she had slept with, worried about who she may have infected and wondering if and how she should contact them to warn them of the potential danger. Amanda's prison diary was, presumably, never meant for public consumption, but with a certain inevitability, its contents found themselves on the front page of the tabloid newspapers. She was told a few days later that the test was, in fact, negative.

Arguably, opinions on promiscuity should be kept to oneself, but are also very diverse. Who is to say how many sexual partners is too many, or not enough? Who is to say that seven is too many? Raffaele was, apparently, a virgin when he met Amanda. Therefore, when he and Amanda were caught on camera hugging and kissing while looking on at the crime scene, the media would place this squarely at Amanda's feet with Raffaele taking the role of a passive partner. Does anybody know, or indeed care, how many sexual partners Rudy had had at the time of his arrest?

Even the language used when talking about her is casually derogatory, even if it's not intended to be. There is talk of her sexual 'conquests' during her time in Italy, suggesting that the men she was involved with were all passive participants. This term is generally reserved to describe men's conquests over women and when applied to them, implies that we should be congratulating the sexually successful man on some sort of victory. When describing females, we get the impression that they should feel shameful about their wanton behaviour. A man's conquests are proof of virility, a woman's are terrifying. And what this does, is strengthen the prosecution's argument for a motive to this crime which otherwise seems non-existent. That Amanda had some sort of sexual power over Rudy and Raffaele, and was, through her devious feminine wiles, able to persuade them to help her to murder Meredith.

There is no doubt that the press coverage, particularly in the UK tabloids, played a huge part in people's negative perception of Amanda Knox. Quite apart from the misinformation being given directly to the press by the Italian police, resulting in some very early news reports relaying that 'forensic experts found Knox's hand imprint on Meredith's face', and that 'cameras overlooking the house in Perugia have captured the 20-year-old American student'[15] entering the cottage on the night of the murder, Amanda was lambasted in one particular newspaper, the *Daily Mail* who updated on the case daily, despite no really new evidence coming to light. Nick Pisa, a journalist for the *Mail* at the time who could speak Italian and therefore had a distinct advantage over his peers, was clearly instrumental in getting the media storm going and, more importantly, the portrayal of Amanda as a sex-crazed devil.

During the 2016 Netflix documentary in which he is interviewed, he describes her getting her 'hooks into' Raffaele due to his 'lack of sexual experience'. He, either deliberately or otherwise, paints himself as almost a pantomime villain, gleefully explaining how the case when it broke was a dream to journalists, including 'everything you could ask for in a story. Blood everywhere. Girl on girl crime.' He does at least have the grace to look slightly embarrassed when he admits that getting this scoop, well, 'I'd like to say it was like having sex.'[16]

Other headlines during the investigation constantly reference Amanda Knox's sexuality, claiming that she 'developed a deep, abiding desire for casual sex', or in other words, was a 'man eater'.[17] The language used is consistently misogynistic; her 'seven lovers' portrayed as a huge number to be ashamed of, she's sex-crazed, she's drug addled, she's promiscuous, she has 'conquests' over men as though they are powerless to resist.

Pisa admits that most of his information was leaked by the police, including her diary with the list of her sexual partners following the false revelation that she was HIV positive, concluding proudly that, 'I was probably one of the first people to get hold of it'. Of course, he explains, he couldn't possibly betray his 'journalistic principles' by revealing his sources. In fact, and probably in fairness, he does call out the people who criticise him for these actions while simultaneously trawling the papers for every possible detail, but he ultimately blames the police for the media frenzy. As he puts it, 'looking back, some of the information that came out was just crazy really, and just completely made up'. Despite knowing this, he admits that he rarely fact-checked anything he was told in his rush to get to print and avoid his rivals stealing his big scoop.

When asked why so much emphasis was placed on her rather than the others, he replied tellingly that, 'nobody was really that bothered about Rudy. I mean obviously we gave it the cursory coverage [but at the end of the day] there was no interest in him.'[18] Amanda was simply much more interesting.

The First Round

So, in contrast to Rudy's under-the-radar, expeditious trial, Amanda and Raffaele's first fully public proceedings would last for over a year; it's entirely usual in the Italian system for court to be in session perhaps only once or twice a week, with a long summer break; in this case from 19 July – 14 September 2009.

The lengthy process began when the prosecution was ready to state their case on 16 January 2009 at the Court of Assizes of Perugia in front of presiding judge Dr Giancarlo Massei, secondary judge Dr Beatrice Cristiani, and a randomly computer-selected six-person jury. Although the trial would be open to the public, it was agreed that out of respect for Meredith, the public would not be allowed in court whenever any images of her body were shown.

The key players at the trial were the aforementioned judges and jury, with prosecutors Mignini and Comodi putting forward the case against the defendants. Amanda's lawyers were English-speaking Carlo Dalla Vedova and local Italian Luciana Ghirga, who spoke no English. Raffaele's lawyers were widely seen as a powerhouse due largely to the funds available to him through his father's wealth. They consisted of Giulia Bongiorno, Marco Brusco and Luca Maori. Patrick's legal representative in the slander element of the trial was Carlo Pacelli. The lawyers representing the Kercher family were Francesco Maresca and Serena Perna.

The trial proceeded at a steady pace and throughout February the early witnesses were called; Laura and Filomena, Meredith's British friends, the *Polizia Postale* and the members of the *Squadra Mobile* who had been first on the scene. This was key particularly for the prosecution, where the subject of the timing of Raffaele's calls to the

Carabinieri was raised, alongside Amanda's behaviour immediately after the murder and throughout the following days and weeks. A timeline of events was beginning to be established and questions asked about the red flags which had made an appearance during this time.

The key eyewitnesses were called throughout March: the grocer Quintavalle, the Albanian Kokomani and the homeless man Curatolo, alongside Capezzali who had allegedly heard a scream on the night the murder took place. Also testifying was Fabio Gioffredi, who alleged to have seen four people walk out of the cottage on 30 October, one of whom he was 99 per cent sure was Rudy, and realised that the other three were Amanda, Meredith and Raffaele after seeing their faces on the news. All of these eyewitnesses proved positive for the prosecution apart from one, Hekuran Kokomani. He was a risk for them, his testimony having been dismissed as 'irrelevant ravings' by Micheli during Rudy's trial and the surrounding hearings. He wasn't the strongest of witnesses; he insisted on testifying in stilted Italian rather than his native Albanian, his testimony was contradictory and at times bewildering, and he eventually became somewhat of a laughing stock after recalling proudly the story of having thrown handfuls of olives at the woman he identified as Amanda on the night of the alleged incident. Ultimately though, the prosecution was happy that among all the bluster, he had at least cast doubt on Amanda and Raffaele's alibi.

The day on which Rudy was called to the stand, 4 April 2009, was much anticipated by both the prosecution and the defence. Everyone hoped that he might shed some more light on the events of that night and perhaps even admit to his part in the murder. They would, however, be disappointed as he exercised his right not to answer any questions at all and ultimately, he was only present in court for a matter of minutes. Amanda and Raffaele both responded in frustration about their inability to be allowed to question him about his version of events and defend themselves against his allegations.

The court took a day trip out on 18 April when they visited the crime scene at No. 7, Via della Pergola, allowing the jury to assess for themselves whether or not they thought that someone, specifically Rudy, could have scaled the wall and entered the building through Filomena's bedroom window, and also if they felt that there was sufficient room in Meredith's still blood-soaked bedroom for three perpetrators to carry out an attack on the victim. The prosecution would claim this visit as a success, with at one stage seven people being present in the room, albeit standing together rather than recreating an attack, and that on viewing the exterior of the window leading into Filomena's room, at least some of the jurors were sceptical about anyone's ability to scale the wall.

The key evidence, however, was forensic and centred mainly on the knife, the bra clasp and the blood evidence at the crime scene. By all accounts, Stefanoni's testimony was incredibly technical, where she explained every trace found at the scene and how each of them pointed definitively to the defendants' guilt. In retaliation, Raffaele's lawyers attacked the bra clasp evidence and Amanda's team did the same with the knife evidence, with both accusing the original forensic teams of shoddy work and suggesting that contamination was probable. The prosecution strenuously denied this, proclaiming indignantly that 'DNA doesn't have wings!'[1] implying that Raffaele's DNA did not simply appear on the bra clasp, it was there for one reason only – because he had touched it.

In terms of the murder weapon, they asserted that the large knife was compatible with some of the wounds inflicted on Meredith but not with some of the other, smaller ones which they say suggested the use of two different knives. This in turn gave weight to the assertion that more than one assailant was involved in the murder. Following on from the forensic testimony and throughout June 2009 the court heard testimony from Arline, Meredith's mother, Amanda and Raffaele's parents and Amanda herself.

This testimony was, of course, the most hotly anticipated of all and began on 12 June with an interrogation by Pacelli about her false accusation of his client, Patrick Lumumba. Then followed questioning by her own lawyer, Ghirga, followed by prosecutors Mignini and Comodi, then Maresca, and lastly Massei. Her testimony took place over two days, and she switched between testifying in English and Italian, the latter of which she had become more fluent in during her time in prison awaiting trial.

Pacelli pressed her about why she had named Patrick and she reiterated again about her alleged treatment at the hands of the police that night. Her testimony when questioned by Ghirga was, of course, designed to confirm her version of events leading up to and after the murder. Mignini's cross examination would prove tougher. It was a tense and stilted affair, with constant interruptions from the defence lawyers causing Mignini to become increasingly frustrated with the process. He also initially focused on her accusation of Patrick, and then moved on to various issues relating to the discovery of the body with the aim of establishing that, right off the bat, Amanda's behaviour had been suspect.

Maresca, questioning on behalf of the Kercher family, focused on Amanda's perceived inappropriate behaviour following the death of her friend. Judge Massei was the last to question her, asking if Meredith had ever visited Raffaele's home, and other questions relating to their mobile phone and computer use, and the order in which the phone calls took place on 2 November before Meredith's body was found. It's widely agreed that his questioning of her was relentless, possibly more so than Mignini's. He surprised everyone by asking her about the temperature in the cottage at No. 7, Via della Pergola before it became apparent that he was suggesting to her that if it was cold, then the decision to go back there to shower rather than stay at Raffaele's that morning was a strange if not suspicious one.

Throughout June and July Raffaele's and Amanda's independent forensics experts, Francesco Introna and Carlo Torre, put forward their review findings for the defence. Introna challenged the time of death, and through his own reconstruction asserted that the knife in evidence could not have been the murder weapon and Meredith had not died in the way that the prosecution described; her room was simply too small for three attackers, and he asserted that Meredith had been killed by a lone attacker. His version has an attacker grabbing Meredith from behind, silencing her with a hand over her mouth before pushing her to the ground and immobilising her with his legs before cutting her throat. While Torre did not share this view, he did agree that the knife was not, in his opinion, the correct size to have caused the fatal wounds and should therefore not be assumed to be the murder weapon. Presently more experts were called for the defence to challenge the admissibility of the DNA evidence, following which both defendants appealed for a full review of the forensic evidence. On 9 October, following the summer recess, their request was turned down. Following this blow to the defence, the prosecution began their closing arguments in November 2009.

The court was treated to a compelling animation containing avatars of the three suspects and the victim which recreated in great detail the prosecution's version of events that night, including superimposed shots of the actual crime scene to cement their theory about how Meredith was actually killed and how the footprints came to be where they were found. The defence's closing arguments contained a combination of measured rebuttal of the forensic evidence and on a more emotional level, gave an insight into the couples' personalities; at odds with what the jury had been led to believe of them.

The long-awaited verdict was announced on 4 December 2009, almost exactly two years and one month since Meredith's murder. Although both defendants had been hopeful that their attack on the forensic evidence would hold some sway with the judges and jury, they were to be disappointed. They were both found guilty of murder, illegally carrying a knife, sexual assault and simulation of a crime. Amanda was also found guilty of *calunnia* against Patrick. They were both acquitted of the charge of stealing Meredith's money but were found guilty of stealing her phones. Amanda was sentenced to twenty-six years in prison, Raffaele to twenty-five.

In the meantime, Rudy was already in his own process of appeal. In November 2009 he pled his case to the appeal court and on 22 December, just a couple of weeks after Amanda and Raffaele had been found guilty, his sentence was reduced from thirty to sixteen years. Appeal for Amanda and Raffaele themselves was, of course, inevitable. Under Italian law the presiding judge must deliver a report on their findings of the case within ninety days of the verdict, after which the defence would be allowed to file an appeal within forty-five days. And so, on 4 March 2010, the Massei report was released, at which point the wheels for appeal were set in motion.

A date for the appeal to begin was set for 24 November 2010 at the Court of Assizes of Appeal of Perugia and again, it would last for almost a year, with a summer break from 30 July to 23 September 2011. This case was presided over by Judge Claudio Pratillo Hellman and secondary Judge Massimo Zanetti, again alongside a jury of six.

In the Italian legal system, an appeal essentially consists of a full retrial, with the prosecution again presenting their case, but for this trial two key things would ultimately change the outcome for Amanda and Raffaele. First, the defence were granted a fresh, independent review of the DNA evidence on the knife, and the bra clasp which had previously been denied during the first trial. Second, they were granted the right to bring new witnesses and to recall Antonio Curatolo, one of the prosecution's original eyewitnesses who testified that he had seen Amanda and Raffaele near the cottage on the night of the murder.

He was called to the stand in March 2011, and his testimony would arguably present a blow to the prosecution; he was obviously confused about dates, particularly which day Halloween fell on, casting doubt on how accurate his original testimony had been. Originally, he had said he had seen the couple on the 1 November, the day of the murder, when they claimed to have been in Raffaele's apartment, and now he said he had seen them on Halloween night itself – although he then stated that he thought Halloween was on 1 or 2 November. Despite this, he did slightly redeem his testimony by remembering that it had been raining when he saw them, when no rain fell on the night of 31 October; his confusion, however, was enough to spark the slightest of doubts.

Throughout June 2011 the defence called their new star witnesses: Mario Alessi, Marco Castelluccio and Luciano Aviello. This choice would prove to be contentious, and indeed the prosecution did not seem duly concerned about their efficacy; they were a group of convicted criminals who had been called to testify about various conversations they claim to have heard in prison. Their testimony, and the witnesses themselves, were treated with barely concealed contempt by the prosecution.

Alessi, a convicted child killer, testified that Rudy had confessed to him in prison that Amanda and Raffaele had nothing to do with the murder; in fact, he said, it had been committed by Rudy's friend who was known only as 'The Drunkard', and that Rudy had been an innocent bystander who had tried to save Meredith's life. Castelluccio was next; he was another prisoner who claimed that he had overheard Rudy admit that the couple were innocent. Lastly, Aviello, yet another convicted criminal, claimed that all three were innocent and that in fact his brother was the culprit; he and a friend had killed Meredith during a botched robbery.

The prosecution felt rightly confident in their cross examination of these three; Maresca played heavily on the child that Alessi had been convicted of murdering to damage his reliability as a witness in the eyes of the jury. Their trump card, however, was bringing Rudy back in to testify on 27 June. He denied everything that the witnesses had said and for the first time, openly asserted that Amanda and Raffaele had killed Meredith. While this was a blow, ultimately the testimony of these new witnesses would have little to do with the outcome of the appeal.

The most successful evidence for the defence was given by Carla Vecchiotti and Stefano Conti, the independent specialists in forensic evidence who had carried out the review of the original results. They stated that the collection of evidence had been severely compromised and pointed out more than fifty failings in a video taken of the original team collecting evidence at the crime scene, which had been shown during the first trial. Understandably the original forensic team took great offence at this attack on their reputation and working methods during the investigation and stood by their original evidence.

Following the impassioned summing-up by both prosecution and defence, on 4 October 2011, Judge Hellman and the court found in favour of Amanda and Raffaele; they had won their appeal against the murder charge. However, Amanda's conviction for the slander of Patrick Lumumba was upheld and she was ordered to pay him damages and was sentenced to three years and eleven days for this crime. Having already spent four years in prison, she was now free to go, as was Raffaele. Amanda immediately returned home with her family to Seattle to a tearful hero's press conference welcome.

Probable Identity

And so, the first round of conviction and acquittal was complete. Of course, this abridged narrative of both trials does not discuss every piece of evidence, nor relate every testimony given. However, it is a matter of fact that there are certain pieces of key evidence, mainly forensic, which are revisited time and time again when discussing this case and which first won, and then ultimately lost, the case for the prosecution. It is fascinating to compare how the Massei and Hellman reports viewed and interpreted these pieces of key evidence in such opposing ways, perhaps strengthening the idea that the validity of evidence can be most certainly open to interpretation.

And so, as Massei had in 2010, presiding Judge Hellman was now required to produce a report to confirm the findings of the case, which was released in December 2011, directly contradicting Massei's findings on many points.

The forensic evidence in this case is arguably the most persuasive, from all sides of the argument, in proving either guilt or innocence in the involvement of the murder on the part of Amanda and Raffaele. Of course, forensics were vital in convicting Rudy Guede and, despite contention still remaining for some about his actual involvement in the murder itself, nobody, including Rudy himself, denies that the DNA evidence placed him at the scene. Although it's very easy for internet sleuths to interpret evidence they discover online, during the trial, Stefanoni's explanation of the DNA evidence was apparently 'sometimes so technical it was difficult for the court to grasp',[1] which does beg the question as to why anyone looking at this evidence second hand on the internet feels they know better than the experts – whether it be on the side of the defence or the prosecution. Nevertheless, they continue to do so.

The murder weapon

First, and surely most important in proving a case against the defendants, must be the positive identification of the murder weapon, and the subsequent linking of that weapon to one or more of the accused. On the face of it, if these two things can be successfully achieved then it's incredibly difficult to refute the outcome. But of course, as with everything in this case, no matter how confidently the case is put, the answer is not as black and white as it appears.

Essentially, during the first trial the prosecution succeeded in proving that the knife they believed to be the murder weapon could be forensically linked to both the victim, Meredith, and one of the accused, Amanda. The link to Raffaele was of course that it was found in the cutlery drawer in his apartment. The 31cm-long knife was taken from the drawer by Inspector Finzi, who says that the knife was laying on top of the other knives; he took only this knife, without touching any other cutlery in the drawer, and chose it because it looked extremely clean.

Stefanoni testified that the knife contained traces of Meredith's DNA on the blade, and of Amanda's on the handle. The defence asserted that the sample was so small that it should not have been introduced into evidence and could easily have been the result of contamination brought about through shoddy handling.

What was contained in the actual samples themselves seems to take on less significance than how they came to be found on the knife blade and handle. The sample, particularly that purported to contain Meredith's DNA, was, in layman's terms, tiny; it was large enough to be tested once, but not sufficient to be retested in an attempt to replicate the first result. In fact, the results themselves were not actually proven to be blood, but rather an organic matter which may or may not have been blood. Given the size of the sample, Stefanoni had opted for establishing who the sample had come from, not the substance from which it came. However, Massei confirmed the prosecution's stance: no matter how small, and what the actual makeup of the sample was, it could not have got onto the knife in any scenario other than through contact with Meredith. She had never visited Raffaele's flat, and therefore at some point the knife must have been present in No. 7, Via della Pergola. Given that Amanda is highly likely to have used the knife during some visit to Raffaele's and while preparing a meal for the pair, the presence of her DNA on the knife would have been irrelevant had it not been for the presence also of Meredith's DNA.

So, the Massei report not only upheld the DNA evidence of Meredith and Amanda on the knife, but systematically debunked any suggestion of contamination, confirming the testimony that the knife was immediately placed in a new paper envelope and then into a folder, and returned to the Police Headquarters. It refutes the possibility put forward by the defence that the knife could have been contaminated either by Superintendent Gubbiotti, to whom the knife was handed when it was delivered from the flat (he having previously been at the crime scene, where he may have picked up traces of Meredith and Amanda's DNA and transferred them), or from flaking skin cells belonging to Meredith which Amanda could have picked up from their shared home, and transferred to the knife at Raffaele's apartment.

The court concluded that these hypotheses were impossible; Gubbiotti had been wearing gloves in the flat, and had changed to a new, clean pair when he took possession of the knife. They found the idea that Amanda had managed to pick up flaked traces of Meredith in the cottage, travelled to Raffaele's flat without touching anything, and then immediately making a beeline for the knife and grasping this first, before anything else, highly improbable, if not impossible.

Hellman's report disagrees. While reiterating that the results were obtained by methods which could not be repeated, in essence it says that without the relevant expertise this minutia of scientific detail is too complicated for one judge to make a decision upon. The defence, it says, should have been allowed an independent review right from the start to counter this issue. Its conclusion is that the analyses performed on the knife blade pertaining to Meredith's sample were not reliable as they did not confirm the presence of blood, and that as it was a low copy number sample (too small to be tested more than once), it could not be validated by international protocols. Ultimately, the Hellman report did not agree that this sample was certain to belong to Meredith, and that the issue of contamination could not be ruled out.

Questions are also asked about the validity of the knife as the murder weapon; why would the killer bring a knife to the scene rather than use one which was already in the cottage? Does the size and shape of the knife fit the wounds? Does it fit the bloody imprint of a knife found on Meredith's bedsheets? The answer to the last question is no, according to the Hellman report, which states that 'a bloody print was found which clearly corresponds to a smaller knife'.[2] This report also states that 'there remains in reality no objective element signifying the fact accepted [by the Court of first instance] that the above-mentioned knife was used in committing the murder'.[3] In short, there is no proof that this was the murder weapon, so the fact that Meredith's DNA was discovered on it is irrelevant.

The Hellman report also suggests that during the first trial, the prosecution were fixated on the knife being the murder weapon, and that because there was evidence that a smaller knife was used during the murder (which was never found and so therefore could not be tested for DNA), they were forced to come up with the 'multiple attacker' theory in order to allow for the larger knife to be confirmed as the murder weapon, alongside a smaller, undiscovered one.

As to how the knife got from Raffaele's flat to No. 7, Via della Pergola in the first place, the prosecution's version is that Amanda carried it with her from Raffaele's flat, in her spacious handbag, for protection against potential attackers during the journey. Hellman casts doubt on this version of events, suggesting that the prosecution claimed the knife was deemed to be the murder weapon, despite a certain difficulty in explaining how it had come to be in the cottage, suggesting that he did not agree with their hypothesis about Amanda carrying it there herself.

The bra clasp

The bra clasp DNA evidence linking Raffaele to the crime scene is perhaps the most contentious, due to the way in which the sample was handled, and the fact that this handling was captured for all to see on video. Firstly, the damning evidence that links Raffaele was that his DNA was found on the hooks of the bra clasp. This particular piece of material had been torn or cut from the rest of the bra, apparently after an abortive attempt to undo it during the course of the murder. On examination, Stefanoni found traces of Raffaele and Meredith on the sample, and traces from Rudy close to where it had been cut away from the rest of the bra.

On the face of it, and similar to the knife DNA evidence, this appears to be cut and dried and was upheld during the first trial as proof of his involvement. The defence, however, had serious issues with the way in which this sample was handled and collected, maintaining that the sloppy way in which this was carried out seriously compromised the sample and rendered it inadmissible.

So what happened to the piece of clasp? According to the Massei report, this sample was first seen during the initial crime scene investigation on 2 November. It was discovered underneath Meredith's body and was not documented separately, but rather 'counted along with the letter indicating the bra'.[4] In other words, it was considered as the same sample as the rest of the bra and was missed at the time and left at the crime scene, even though the other part of the sample (the rest of the bra) was taken away for examination that day. It was discovered again during another visit to the crime scene on 18 December, around 1.5 metres away from where it had first been discovered. This time, it was partially hidden by a rug and a sock.

The Massei report describes what happens next: it was 'collected, photographed, repositioned on the floor, taken up again, observed and placed in the envelope which was then sealed and sent to the laboratory for analyses'.[5] This might be described as a slight underplaying of what was witnessed on the video footage of the discovery, where we can see an investigator pick up the clasp, hand it to his colleague who shines a torch on it, and in doing so drops it on the floor. He then retrieves it, places it on the floor where it is photographed, and then hands it back to his colleague who places it in an evidence bag.

On the back of this, the defence argue that this sample could have been contaminated at multiple times during its time in the cottage. The Massei report refuted this, saying that the hypothetical transfer of Raffaele's DNA to the clasp was simply a general complaint by the defence; just because the clasp had been left for forty-six days and then handled by several people (allegedly wearing dirty gloves) meaning that there is a *possibility* of transfer, doesn't mean it happened; the defence were merely speculating without coming up with specific proof of contamination taking place.

But exactly how could this contamination have happened? The prosecution asserted that the only way Raffaele's DNA could have got on the clasp would have been by him grasping it firmly (presumably in the act of attempting to remove it). The Massei report, as with the knife evidence, debunked any scenario in which his DNA might otherwise have got there. Contamination from Raffaele himself after the body was discovered? No, he was nowhere near the body when it was found, and after leaving the cottage never entered it again. Left his DNA in the house on a previous visit which was then transferred to the bra clasp? No, because according to testimony, on every previous visit to the cottage he always stayed close by Amanda's side and never entered Meredith's room and the likelihood of it being transferred anyway is extremely unlikely as 'simple contact between objects does not transfer DNA'. The clasp was admittedly left under a rug for weeks, but even then, actual pressure would have to have been asserted to transfer any DNA from rug/sock to the clasp and Stefanoni testified that the bra clasp's deformation (the hooks were bent when it was first found) had not changed in that time, indicating that no pressure had been put on it in the meantime.

Hellman again disagreed. The bra clasp DNA review was mentioned alongside the knife DNA already discussed and concluded that the technical analysis of the clasp was not reliable. The reasons put forward again cite the inability to follow international protocols for collection and sampling of the exhibit and ruling that some sort of contamination could not be ruled out. In terms of the sample itself, the prosecution had described, again in layman's terms, that it included a Y chromosome which could only have belonged to Raffaele, or a male relative of his. Hellman concluded that this interpretation was erroneous.

The bathroom

On forums and in discussions about the case, perhaps the reason most cited for confirming Amanda's guilt is the mixed DNA evidence.

The prosecution put forward the evidence during the first trial that during their investigation of the bathroom they discovered, among other single traces, mixed biological traces of Amanda and Meredith on the bidet which appeared to have consisted of diluted blood, and the same result from a sample from the basin, and also from the cotton bud box which was sitting on the basin.

The other mixed traces came from the later investigation where Luminol was used to reveal various footprints during which samples discovered in Filomena's room were said to contain a mixed genetic profile of Meredith and Amanda. Simply put, those who believe Amanda to have taken part in this crime say that this is incontrovertible evidence that she was involved; after all, her DNA didn't simply fly into Filomena's room and happen to land on top of Meredith's DNA. The only explanation is that she was in the cottage when Meredith was murdered.

With regards to the bathroom evidence, Massei concluded that the only way the blood could have been mixed together would have been during a scenario whereby Amanda entered the bathroom with Meredith's blood on her hands. In doing so she left Meredith's blood on the light switch, and on the right-hand edge of the door (where traces of Meredith's single blood samples were found). The presence of the bloody footprint on the bathmat assumes that whoever entered the bathroom had the victim's blood on them, and therefore their purpose of entering was to wash themselves. It asserts that the mixed traces were left during the process of washing their hands in the basin.

Hellman countered that this evidence is simply irrelevant. It was confirmed that there was no way of determining the age of the specimen or indeed the order in which they were left (i.e., Meredith's blood could theoretically have been left on the basin months ago, with Amanda's added weeks later; there is no way of knowing for sure) and that, as both women shared a bathroom, the likelihood of their mixed traces being there was high, if not inevitable. However,

Massei had previously decreed that the mixed trace specimens were in fact deposited simultaneously, and by Amanda.

In terms of the blood in the bathroom, the question of the samples' validity essentially came down to their method of collection; the samples were collected on the same piece of blotting paper and collected in a dragging, wiping motion rather than a dabbing motion, leading to the conclusion that the traces could well have been mixed together in this way on collection, and not during a clean up after a murder.

Feet

An awful lot of evidence in this case seems to revolve around feet, be it bare footprints or those made by various shoes. First, a total of eleven shoe prints were analysed, which had been found during the initial investigations of the crime scene between 2 to 5 November. They consisted of five prints found in the living room, two in the hallway just in front of Meredith's bedroom door, and three found in Meredith's bedroom near her body and were all confirmed to have contained blood. Other prints tested included a latent print found on a pillowcase underneath Meredith's body and two dust footprints found in Filomena's room, on postcards on the floor.

Police tested these prints against four shoes: a size nine Nike Air Force 1 belonging to Raffaele, a size seven Skechers belonging to Amanda, and a size ten Adidas Universal and size eleven Timberland boot, both belonging to Rudy. During a search of Rudy's house on 21 November, investigators had discovered an empty shoe box for a Nike Outbreak shoe, size eleven; the actual shoes themselves were never found, but an identical and brand-new pair were purchased for the purposes of testing.

Initially, and before Rudy was a suspect, police believed that one of the prints found near Meredith's body belonged to Raffaele.

However, once the Nike Outbreak shoes came onto the scene, further testing confirmed that the 'probable identity' of the wearer was Rudy; the use of the word 'probable' being because the original shoes were never found, or indeed entered into evidence. Of the prints which were able to be used in evidence, all concluded that the 'probable identity' was that of Rudy Guede. However, of particular interest was the print on the pillowcase discovered under Meredith's body. Following testing it was determined that it did not match any of the shoes being used for testing. Size wise, it was hypothesised that it belonged to a woman, based on the heel measurements and overall dimensions which were consistent with an EU shoe size of around thirty-six to thirty-eight (the equivalent to a US size six to seven-and-a-half). This print is considered useful for negative comparisons only, but of course, brings with it much speculation. It cannot be proven, but those who think Amanda is guilty are convinced that this print belongs to her; her Skechers were a size seven and the print was found underneath Meredith's body, so it was unlikely to have been made during the initial discovery of the body and therefore begs the question: to who else it could conceivably belong?

However, in court, Raffaele's independent forensic consultant argued that the print could have been made by Rudy's right foot, reconciling the imprint with Rudy's Nike Outbreaks. The opposing conclusions come from the fact that the forensic investigators posit that the print was made by the 'heel and middle part of the sole of a left shoe', as opposed to the 'part of the foot positioned near the heel rather than to that part from the forefoot'.[6] If the defence is correct, this goes some way to strengthen the idea that Rudy acted alone.

While the shoe print evidence arguably doesn't hurt Amanda and Raffaele's defence (and in fact strengthens the case against Rudy), the footprints allegedly made in blood which showed up during the forensic testing made on 18 December were potentially far more damning. As well as shoe prints to examine, investigators also had several bare footprints to consider. In the same way that they compared shoes taken from the suspects with the shoe prints found, they took footprints from each suspect using inking technology with printers' ink to create a comparison with the evidence found. Each footprint discovered had been made by a right foot, so prints were taken of Rudy, Raffaele and Amanda's right feet on 12 May 2008.

Possibly the most talked about footprint is the one made in blood on the shower mat; partly because of its ability to potentially identify the killer, and partly because of the fact that Amanda ignored it, stepping over it in order to take a shower on the morning of 2 November. In terms of its forensic importance though, it was one of the first pieces of footprint evidence discovered during the initial crime scene inspection between 2–5 November. It is a partial print, showing the big toe, metatarsal and partial plantar arch of a right foot.

The validity of this evidence essentially boils down to measurements, and their accuracy or inaccuracy. During the first trial, where Raffaele and Amanda were found guilty, the prosecution asserted that the 'probable identity' of the footprint belonged to Raffaele. In the same way that the print found on Meredith's pillowcase was determined to be useful only for negative comparison, the same was said of the bloody footprint on the bathmat. Its size rules Amanda out, so the footprint was compared to the ink prints of both Raffaele and Rudy, and, in layman's terms, the measurements were closer to Raffaele's than Rudy's, thus probable identity was ascertained. As one expert pointed out, an exact match could never be made given that the original was made in blood on a towelling bathmat and the reference point taken in ink on paper. Because the measurements of the bloody footprint were closer to Raffaele's, although not an exact match, they were deemed to be consistent, compared to less consistency with the measurements of Rudy's foot.

The defence argued that the measurements taken from the bathmat were inaccurate, with the original reference points being taken from the wrong place resulting in a mismeasurement of over five millimetres, bringing the big toe measurement more in line with Rudy's dimensions.

So essentially, Massei concluded the compatibility on Raffaele's big toe and overall foot being wider that Rudy's narrower sample, in line with the measurements taken from the mat. During the final appeals more technical measurements would be discussed but for now, Hellman concluded that investigators had not sufficiently explored the possibility of the footprint belonging to Rudy and puts forward a hypothesis that he may have lost his right shoe during the murder, thus walking barefoot into the bathroom and leaving an imprint in Meredith's blood on the shower mat during his attempt to clean himself up.

As for the prints allegedly made in blood which showed up following the Luminol test they seemed to consist of five main samples:

- One footprint inside Amanda's bedroom
- Two footprints in the hallway facing the exit
- One shoe print in the hallway facing the exit
- One footprint in the hallway facing towards the entrance to Meredith's room.

Unlike the print on the bathmat, which was photographed next to a measure for reference, these prints were not, as through necessity the photographs were taken in darkness. The way in which this is overcome is that reference photos are taken in the light for comparison, on exactly the same spot. The defence would argue that the measurements were not accurate, that the photos had not been taken at ninety degrees to the floor and therefore may be subject to perspective correction, leading to a slight change in measurements. However, the similarities with the other shoe print evidence are that all of the useable prints were deemed useful for negative comparison only. The shoe print was not deemed useful for any comparison, and nor was the left footprint in the hallway. However, during the first trial the print outside Amanda's bedroom and the one outside Meredith's room were deemed to be compatible with Amanda's right foot. The right footprint in the hallway was deemed to be compatible with Raffaele's right foot. As with the bathmat footprint, the larger footprint was deemed to belong to Raffaele as the measurements fitted his foot more closely than Rudy's.

This probable identification would seem to be, if not incontrovertible proof, then at least very damning; it suggests that both Amanda and Raffaele were walking around the apartment that evening with blood on their feet, and not only that, but they made the effort to clean up after themselves, as the footprints were not visible to the naked eye. However, the defence, and the Hellman report would disagree, and their argument is not necessarily that the footprints don't belong to the accused (although they do doubt the accuracy of the measurements) but more to the point that the footprints were not conclusively made in blood.

By Massei's admission, the samples were 'invisible to the naked eye' and 'meagre/scant/slight', and were not proven to be made up of blood or a substance containing blood. In fact, a 'generic diagnosis for blood had been performed and had given a negative result', and therefore 'it could not be said with certainty that blood was present in the material'.[7] However, Massei ascertains that in all probability the substance was blood, as opposed to other organic traces which can be picked up by Luminol, for example rust, fruit juice, bleach or vegetable matter. The reason why the blood test had come up negative was due to the fact that Stefanoni had chosen to concentrate the tests on the meagre sample she collected to ascertain to whom they belonged, and not the substance of which they consisted.

Massei decreed as highly improbable the defence's suggestion that these prints could quite easily have been made in, for example, fruit juice spilled at any time before the murder, which Amanda and Meredith could feasibly have walked into Filomena's room. It conceded that bleach was more probable, but that the theory was not substantiated due to the lack of any smell of bleach when officers first arrived on the scene.

The Hellman report concluded that the assertion that the footprints were made in blood 'faces insurmountable contradiction, both logical and factual'.[8] It disagreed with Stefanoni's idea that she would have to concentrate on the 'who' rather than the 'what' regarding the sample, citing the defence consultant, Professor Tagliabracci, who testified that a positive result could be ascertained with as little as five red blood cells. Therefore, Stefanoni could, and should, have been able to detect blood had it been present; Hellman therefore concluded that these footprints were not, in fact, made in blood. It also put forward the idea that bleach could well have caused the footprints and this, in fact, was a far more likely scenario. With regards to the smell, plenty of products containing bleach are fragranced and would not therefore have given off a strong smell; even if bleach had been used, there is no way of dating when the prints were made and so the smell could have already dissipated.

Hellman also calls into question why, if the prints were made in blood, were they not consecutive but rather, dotted around and only found in a few places around the cottage. If, as the prosecution asserts, they were from Amanda walking blood away from the crime scene, surely there would be many more of them, and showing a more consistent walking pattern. As with the blood on the basin, equally there is no way of knowing when and in which order the samples were placed, and puts forward the suggestion that it may even have been a footprint from Rudy that contaminated Amanda's DNA with Meredith's.

In summing up, the Hellman report effectively said that it was annulling the verdict due to there being reasonable doubt about Amanda and Raffaele's guilt. And so, by 2011, Amanda and Raffaele were officially innocent, although some would say that they were not guilty, rather than innocent, with the conclusion that Rudy had not acted alone still hanging over them.

Reasonable Doubt

And this case was far from over. Both the prosecutors and the Kercher family appealed against Hellman's rulings and in March 2013, Italy's Supreme Court of Cassation annulled the acquittal. The report by Judge Dr Severo Chieffi explaining this decision was published in June 2013 and concluded that the appeal court was wrong, for several reasons.

First, they asserted that Hellman should have agreed that the break-in was staged, and that Curatolo and Quintavalle's testimonies should have held more weight rather than simply being dismissed. In terms of Rudy, Chieffi ruled that the appeal court should have taken into account Rudy's guilty verdict that he did not act alone as being relevant to their case, and that Rudy's initial statement that Amanda had nothing to do with it should not have been assigned any value at all. Essentially, their point was that if Amanda and Raffaele assert that Rudy shouldn't be believed when he states that Raffaele was there in the cottage that night, why should he then be believed when he says Amanda was not?

It ruled that Amanda's handwritten *memoriale* should have been evaluated in more detail, not holding with the ruling that this was written under psychological pressure given that it was written voluntarily, after her interrogation. It therefore concluded that Amanda's statements and behaviour should have been more prominently used, stating as an example her description of Meredith's body in the wardrobe despite not having seen it first-hand and also the fact that she called home to her mother at 12.47pm when no crime had as yet been discovered.

Chieffi disagreed with Hellman about the time of death, the assertion that Rudy somehow lost his right shoe during the murder and that the mixed blood evidence was inadmissible. He was also scathing about the defence's assertion that the DNA evidence could have been contaminated, wanting to see concrete proof rather than mere speculation.

The conclusion was that another new trial would begin on 30 September 2013 at the Second Court of Assizes Appeal of Florence. During this trial, which would ultimately last until 20 January 2014, the pair were re-convicted; Raffaele was present during the proceedings, but Amanda did not attend, still being in residence back in Seattle. The former, who was still resident in Italy, was ordered to turn in his passport but Amanda was, for the moment, safe from extradition as under Italian law, there is still a presumption of innocence until every appeal has been exhausted.

Judge Alessandro Nencini had presided over this retrial, and his motivation report was released on 29 April 2014 and broadly agreed with the original Massei verdict.

Of course, the story was not over yet. In 2015 Amanda and Raffaele lodged what would be their final appeal to the Supreme Court of Cassation and following a review, their convictions were overturned for the final time on 27 March 2015, presided over by Judge Gennaro Marasca.

Marasca's report relays a full summary of the previous three verdicts and then goes on to explain Amanda and Raffaele's points of contention put forward in their appeal, followed by the findings and reasonings of the court. Amanda's team put forward the following points: first, that the prosecution had failed to provide an adequate motive for her involvement in the crime. They then cited several forensic issues: the incorrect interpretation of the scientific results due to the absence of repeatable testing on the knife; the potential contamination due to the incorrect handling of the knife and bra clasp; and finally, they asserted that the knife was not proven to be the actual murder weapon. They argued that the evidence about the genetic traces was inconsistent and inaccurate, and that ultimately not a single trace of Amanda's DNA was discovered in the room where the murder took place.

With regards to Rudy, they put forward that cuts on his hands implicating him in the breaking of the window glass to gain entry were not considered fully enough, and nor was his criminal record which proved that he had used a similar method of gaining entry to other properties in the past. They also called into question the interpretation of Rudy's conversations before his arrest and asserted that the stolen phones were found in a place consistent with Rudy's route home from the cottage, which should also have been taken into consideration. They called into question the reliability of the evidence regarding where each of the phone calls had been made, and the inadequacy of the report into the damage done to Raffaele's computer.

Perhaps most prominently, and because Amanda was also appealing against her *calunnia* charge, they also asserted that her unstable psychological condition had not (but should have been) taken into consideration, and that her declarations should have been inadmissible.

Raffaele's team put forward many more reasons than Amanda's, but clearly many that overlapped with hers, including: the lack of proven motive; that there was no trace of him in the room where the murder took place; a general agreement on the handling of the knife and bra clasp, and the subsequent inadequacy of the testing; and an assertion that the knife was not in fact the murder weapon, not least because it was incompatible with the wounds inflicted on Meredith.

Interestingly, and perhaps because, theoretically, Raffaele's potential alibi was easier to prove by use of his computer records, many of the points his team make are regarding the time of death.

He asserts that the previous trial had ignored his alibi based on his computer records but more importantly, that they should have placed much more emphasis on the need to establish Meredith's time of death more accurately. According to Meredith's phone records, they assert that the time of death should have been established as happening between 9.00pm and 10.13pm, because at the time a text message was received on her phone at 10.13pm, the handset was established as being in the garden where it was found the following day – the implication being that Meredith must already have been dead by then. At 8.56pm a call had been placed to her home number in England, implying that she was still alive just before 9.00pm.

Raffaele asserts that computer records prove that he watched a cartoon on his computer at 9.26pm which lasted for twenty minutes, placing him at home until 9.46pm. These timings put Curatolo's testimony in doubt as he claimed to have seen the pair between 9.30pm and 12.30am. The scream Capezzali heard was at 11.00pm or 11.30pm, by which time Meredith was already dead, rendering this evidence useless. In a similar vein, they call into question the validity of all the eyewitness accounts, on the grounds that they had been produced some time after the fact and only then because a journalist, Fois, had sought out the story.

Several of Raffaele's team's issues revolve around requests for various testing, which were all denied. Specifically, a sperm sample found on a pillow in Meredith's room, new IT analysis of his computer, and a review of how on earth it might be possible to remove all traces of Raffaele and Amanda, while leaving just Rudy's DNA present. They also requested examination of the stone found in Filomena's room in case Rudy's DNA might have been found on it (or perhaps to rule out his own), audiometric tests to ascertain if Capezzali would have been able to hear the scream from her residence, and a final examination of the bra clasp to cancel out any doubt, all of which were refused.

Raffaele's team also placed a lot of emphasis on the investigation of the alleged staged break-in, asserting that investigators didn't consider important that it was he who first alerted them to the fact that nothing was missing which, if guilty of staging the scene, would have been improbable. As with Amanda, they asserted that the investigators had ignored Rudy's previous similar break-ins, and the cuts on his hands; he also said that they had misinterpreted the evidence of the shards of glass and that some had in fact been found under the pile of clothes as well as on top, and even that a fragment of glass retrieved from Meredith's room had been ignored.

Several other misinterpretations of evidence were also listed: the size thirty-seven footprint; the timing of the 112 calls; that the crime scene had been staged by two people; the illogical reasoning that the alleged murder weapon wouldn't have been hidden somewhere more effective than just being returned to the kitchen drawer – or the assertion that Amanda would have carried it with her to and from the crime scene.

Essentially, both appeals boiled down to the fact that they had been convicted while they are adamant that reasonable doubt was proven over and over again. So, both parties had put forward comprehensive arguments as to why this final appeal should be won, and Marasca agreed – but not without certain conditions. However, the report is full of criticism of the Massei and Nencini verdicts and is at times scathing.

The main points with which the report agreed, on both sides, were that the investigators should have, but failed to, prove a motive for the defendants, specifying that the motive applied to Rudy Guede could not, and should not, also be applied to Amanda and Raffaele. Also, that they had failed to prove that the evidence of guilt was beyond reasonable doubt. Other failings included: being in a rush to conclude the case due to the unusual media attention surrounding it; failing to adhere to the correct sterile procedures; and violating the rules dictated by international protocols, resulting in the genetic testing evidence being useless. The court agreed that investigators should have placed more store in confirming the time of death, and agreed that Meredith was likely already dead by 10.13pm. In fact, they strongly criticised the police on their 'sketchy arithmetic' on this point.

Where the report goes into more detail, however, surrounds the DNA evidence. First, it makes the point that 'there doesn't exist a single science, a bringer of truth',[1] or in other words: a case cannot be decided on one piece of scientific evidence and that the judge, not being a scientific expert, should not be called upon to decide on which of the opposing experts is correct.

It goes on to criticise the collection and handling of both the knife and the bra clasp, reiterating that the knife had been packed in flimsy cardboard, and that the bra clasp had not only been left for forty-six days, but had then been handled with dirty gloves. In terms of the testing, it confirmed that the samples were of low copy number and therefore unable to be replicated and risked producing a false positive result. A judicial error had therefore been made by the previous trial judge who had placed such value on an inadequate test.

Lastly, it confirms as illogical that Amanda and Raffaele would have been able to clean up simply their own biological traces while leaving Rudy's intact and, if they were to have made an attempt at cleaning, they surely would have cleaned up the blood discovered in the small bathroom, not having been in any hurry to leave the scene. It goes so far as to describe as 'ridiculous' the assertion that the footprints discovered by the Luminol were definitely made in blood and not in some sort of bleach-based cleaning fluid. If true, it would, it said, imply that the cottage had never been cleaned, or for that matter, ever even lived in.

The errors in judgement listed led Marasca to conclude that their sentences must be annulled and stated as one reason, the 'absolute absence of biological traces referable to [the defendants] (apart from the hook)',[2] which was dismissed as inadmissible. As there was deemed to be no likelihood of any further evidence coming to light, or indeed of Rudy ever confirming any details of what occurred that night, then the annulment which was decreed was 'without remand', or in other words, was final. No further appeals can take place. Amanda's *calunnia* charge however, still stood.

So, it would seem that this strong criticism of the investigation and the agreement with the majority of the defendants' complaints would be final and conclusive. However, Marasca concludes his report with an interesting assertion, and one which, for those who think that Amanda and Raffaele were involved in this murder, confirms their assertion that they are not, in fact, fully exonerated, but merely that they got away with this crime on a technicality due to shoddy police work.

And this assertion is that, by law, Amanda – and by association Raffaele – were present at the cottage on the night of the murder. This all boils down to the fact that Amanda's conviction for slander still stands, and that therefore her confession where she implicates Patrick and says that she was in the house at the time is a 'proven fact in the trial' and therefore, in the eyes of the law, correct. Essentially, Marasca's report does not agree that this confession was coerced, and therefore, that it is a true statement of fact. The theory that she confessed due to psychological pressure is 'fragile', and her implication of Patrick was theorised as a cover up for Rudy, who she was protecting, in the event that he might retaliate and implicate her. The report very clearly states that this is because, 'Mr Lumumba, like Mr Guede, is a man of colour'.[3]

Marasca goes on to confirm the opinion that Amanda's behaviour and lies were suspicious, but that as Curatolo and Quintavalle had been disregarded as reliable witnesses, no proof was evident. While conceding that her DNA on the knife was of no consequence, being a regular visitor at Raffaele's, and that it was implausible that she would carry the knife to and from the scene, the report does say that although there were no blood stains found on the knife it still could conceivably have been used in the murder.

Lastly, and based on the assertion that Amanda was in the cottage that night, by association they conclude that Raffaele was also present, albeit impossible to prove. Quite apart from the fact that they were lovers and would therefore be likely to have been together, Raffaele received no phone calls from Amanda during the time period she says she was taking a shower at the cottage, implying that he must have been with her at the time. They also say that even if Raffaele had watched a video until 9.46pm he could still have made it to the cottage in time to participate in the murder, and that their mixed-up alibis were ultimately suspicious, describing Raffaele's as, if not false, then at the very least 'unsuccessful'.[4]

So, despite Marasca's initial assertion at the beginning of the report that 'the only fact of irrefutable certainty being the guilt of Amanda Knox regarding the slanderous accusations against Patrick Lumumba', he does then go on to say later that 'the second irrefutable certainty that is the guilt now under irrevocable ruling, of the Ivorian as the author – *participating with others* – of the murder of the young English woman'.[5]

In the same way that Amanda placing herself at the scene of the crime was proven in her *calunnia* sentence, the fact that during Rudy's trial it was confirmed that he didn't act alone is, therefore, in the eyes of Italian law, an undeniable and irrefutable fact.

Therefore, even now that a final verdict is in place, there can still be no agreement between those who think Amanda is innocent and those who think she is guilty. She is either fully exonerated, as the ruling that she was in the house at the time of the murder came about purely as a result of her treatment by police in extracting her statement, or she got away with murder.

BEYOND

Arguing with Strangers on the Internet

Perhaps because of its multi-national nature, this is one of the most high-profile cases still causing arguments more than fifteen years after the crime was committed, and at the time of writing, seven years after the final appeal verdict. On the surface it would seem that those who believe in Amanda and Raffaele's innocence have nothing further to prove following the decision in 2015, but on deeper investigation this doesn't seem to be the case at all.

While no longer claiming front-page status, reports will periodically appear about, for example, Amanda and Raffaele meeting again in Italy, or in a rather more subdued manner, the release of Rudy's book. So where do those people who continue to regularly discuss this case hang out? Firstly, there exist two main websites dedicated to the case: one maintaining Amanda and Raffaele's guilt and the other their innocence. They could be described as a perfect example of confirmation bias at work in that they both discuss the same evidence and yet interpret it in totally opposing ways.

A first glance at *Injustice in Perugia*, a sub-site of *Injustice Anywhere*, an organisation which works to correct wrongful convictions, suggests a line has been drawn under the case with the succinct headline on their home page declaring 'March 27, 2015: Amanda Knox and Raffaele Sollecito have been fully exonerated. There will be no more trials. It's over.'[1] Bruce Fischer, who founded the site in early 2010, also self-published a book by the same name in 2011 which commits the contents of the site to paper.

The site is described as 'a grass roots organisation working to correct the wrongful convictions of Amanda Knox and Raffaele Sollecito', and before the successful appeal, pledged that it 'will not rest until Amanda Knox and Raffaele Sollecito are fully exonerated in Italy'. It is a comprehensive take on the case and, understandably, given its aim, describes the events using very forthright and unambiguous language, an example being its opening statement explaining that 'Meredith Kercher was murdered by Rudy Guede in Perugia Italy, 1 November 2007. Meredith was a beautiful young woman who had her life stolen from her in an act of pure evil. Amanda Knox and Raffaele Sollecito had absolutely nothing to do with her murder. They are both innocent.'[2]

When delving further into both the main site and its file library containing court transcripts and the like, a clear picture emerges about some supporters' views on anyone who dares to suggest that Amanda and Raffaele may, in fact, be guilty. The most telling section entitled, 'The Guilters' [*sic*], shows real animosity towards these foes. In a short but vitriolic passage they describe a 'guilter' as 'someone that believes in the guilt of Amanda Knox and Raffaele Sollecito regardless of any evidence that is presented proving otherwise'. It goes on to explain that 'guilters are people that bought into all of the lies that were leaked to the press from the beginning of the trial to the present. Guilters continue to spread these lies long after they have been completely refuted', and that 'some guilters simply refuse to admit they made a mistake', so will 'lie at all costs to hold on to their precious reputation'.[3]

So, who are these 'guilters'?

The other site chronicling the case goes by the acronym TJMK, or *True Justice for Meredith Kercher*, and was established by Peter Quennell back in 2007, apparently just as the case broke in the news. In an almost mirror image of *Injustice in Perugia*, this one list entries such as 'Amanda's Lies', 'Sollecito's Lies', and a number of posts picking apart both Amanda and Raffaele's books, written since their exoneration. They claim to have extracted '500-Plus Lies in Knox's

Misleading, Defamatory Book', and 'Multiple Lies & Defamations in Sollecito's Book'.[4] Bruce Fischer and Peter Quennell are polar opposites in their views on the case and, understandably, less than glowing in their opinions of each other judging by some of their website content.

TJMK is a forum in itself, with most of its content in blog form, frequently commented on by members, and is described on the Injustice site as 'a discussion board with a disturbing cult like atmosphere'.[5] Whether or not this is true, it's clear that the posters are all very much in favour of Amanda and Raffaele's guilt; it's not clear whether her supporters are allowed to join the forum, but either they aren't, or if they are, their comments are not approved. It certainly puts forward a one-sided view of the case, as of course does its counterpart.

The general ambition of this site is very much to correct the perceived misinformation believed by those who think Amanda is innocent, as they claim that 'the vast majority of authors, journalists and experts who have written about the case have never looked at all case files or noted all the available evidence', and therefore the hope is that 'this file library may help correct some inaccurate perceptions of the case'.[6]

Among the many and varied posts about the case, one in particular stands out: an in-depth analysis of Amanda's written statement from 6 November which, it states, 'points even more strongly toward guilt'.[7] It was posted by Peter Hyatt, who, according to his website, is now a statement analyst who offers 'deception detection training' to law enforcement, or indeed anyone working in 'a field where knowing the truth matters'.[8] It's not clear if this was his profession back in 2010 when the post was written, when he allegedly shared his findings via a blog under a different name. In this post though, he claims to be able to prove that Amanda Knox is guilty of causing or participating in Meredith's death, simply by looking at the phrasing used in her statement, which he implies will override any suggestions of corruption or contamination of evidence; she will tell us in her own words if she is guilty or not.

Hyatt goes on to explain about various deceptive indicators: sensitive words, use of possessive pronouns, passive voice, and 'strong' and 'weak' words; he picks apart Amanda's note with great intensity, for example in reference to her, 'perhaps I made love to Raffaele'. He asks the reader to 'note that she "perhaps" made love', going on to explain that 'this is more than just deceptive: it is an indication of someone else's presence.' It's not entirely clear why, although he explains that by the use of the word 'we' earlier in the sentence, coupled with telling the reader that she made love to him, she is indicating 'the presence, within sexual activity, of more than just Amanda Knox and Raffaele.'

When she explains that she 'smoked marijuana with him' on that night, he asks the reader to 'Note "with him" instead of "Raffaele and I smoked marijuana";' arguing that this phrasing 'shows distance'. During her interrogation, when she says, 'Not only was I told I would be arrested and put in jail for thirty years, but I was also hit in the head when I didn't remember a fact correctly', Hyatt asserts that 'she could have said "I didn't remember a fact" but instead says "I didn't remember a fact correctly" which would show deliberate deception.'

When it comes down to the actual act of murder, Amanda says of Raffaele: 'I don't think he killed Meredith, but I do think he is scared, like me.' Hyatt says that as 'she does not say "Raffaele did not kill Meredith" but only that she does not "think" he did', she is 'leaving room for someone else to "think" otherwise'.

One theme Hyatt returns to repeatedly is that of water, as he claims that 'the element of water is often found in statements where a sexual assault or homicide has taken place'. He leaps on Amanda's mention of showering with Raffaele; 'Note that the entry of water into a statement is often an indicator of sexual assault. Whether it is the washing of clothes, washing of hands, shower, bath, etc', and on this basis goes so far as to claim that 'here we have the first indicator that her roommate died as part of a sexual homicide'. Ultimately, Hyatt stands behind his analysis 100 per cent and claims that 'Amanda Knox, herself, has told us that she was part of a sexual homicide, was present, and that she knows hard evidence thus proves it.'[9]

To say that the 'guilters' and supporters come together to clash on a Reddit sub dedicated to discussing the case would be simplifying the matter, although on this particular forum discussion is often pushed aside to make way for heated arguments.

Reddit describes itself as 'The Front Page of the Internet', and is 'a network of communities based on people's interests'.[10] Essentially it consists of thousands of sub-forums or 'subs', each dedicated to a particular subject where people can discuss topics, ask questions, seek advice or simply share stories. Each sub is prefixed with an r/ and at the time of writing there were around 138,000 active subs on the site, many dedicated to true crime cases.

One is named *r/amandaknox* and describes itself as 'a place to discuss Amanda Knox',[11] without specific inclusion of Raffaele and Rudy in its name – although inevitably many of its discussions revolve around the entire case, and not just Amanda. It was created in April 2014 and at the time of writing has around 1,800 subscribers.

To be clear, the majority of forum members are, while very forthright in their views, rational and polite, and while they may disagree with each other the worst that will happen is a flurry of mild contempt aimed at those who hold views which do not echo their own. However, there are clearly also members whose sole purpose is to look out for 'guilters' and make it their business to patrol the threads to right perceived wrongs. Many polite, interesting and civilised discussions are interspersed with random admonishments such as: 'you have no idea what you are talking about, in any of your terrible posts. You are about the biggest nutter I have seen in this thread', or:

'so you are a nutjob as well that thinks Knox is guilty? Please provide any evidence at all that supports your claim, I guarantee I can refute it or prove it is a lie.'[12]

This goes both ways of course; accusations are thrown around suspecting people of being 'alts' (posting under an alternative profile created for the purpose of giving support to their own posts), some of which even suggest that the more ardent supporters' real identity is that of Edda, Amanda's mother, cruising the sites to correct misinformation from being spread about her daughter. It's hard to tell whether or not this particular accusation is made in jest simply to get a rise out of their foe or an actual belief but honestly, either could be true.

The subjects of the myriad of posts contained in this sub is hugely varied. Questions are asked and heated discussions follow on topics such as the washing discovered in the machine after the murder (was it damp, or simply warm? Did they really forget to throw the bathmat in there?), the alleged clean up (why choose that particular style of mop? Why was Amanda's desk lamp found in Meredith's room?), and if Rudy is telling the truth, why did Amanda ring on the doorbell that night (maybe she forgot her keys? Was there a sliding lock on the door?). These examples are just the tip of the iceberg with most posts involving discussions heading off into incredibly detailed analysis and often degenerating into mudslinging and exchanges of insults generally based on the perceived level of stupidity their opponent is revealing. Discussions often move away from facts, and many are purely speculative, one example being the assertion that Raffaele was released because of his shady father and his alleged links with the mafia, going so far as to assert that Amanda is not strictly innocent, she simply walked free only because of help from the aforementioned illicit gang. Many speculate as to the conversations or thought processes which they feel must have occurred on the part of the suspects, recreating fictional dialogue to hammer home the point.

Worryingly, several people who may not have researched the case quite as thoroughly as others are quite happy to take a stranger's word at face value when looking for answers about the case.

While the minutiae of the discussions involve interpretation of evidence and behaviour, generally the aim is to validate their theories; whether or not Rudy acted alone based on the forensic evidence, which of the three suspects, if any, was lying, and Amanda's erratic behaviour, and her relationship with the two men. There is never any conclusion, as there never can be, but there exists a relentless, repetitive, circular atmosphere due to the fact that, as one member puts it, 'no matter which theory you believe, some things just don't add up'.[13]

Perhaps this is because the word which crops up most often in discussions about this case is 'lie', or more specifically: 'she lied' and 'he lied'. There's no doubt that, whether the reasons were innocent or duplicitous, Rudy, Raffaele and Amanda at the very least changed their story several times throughout the investigation, and at the worst, they lied outright. This seems to form the basis of most discussions on the forums and begs the question: which one of them, if any, do you believe?

One thread asks members to vote in a poll posing the question: 'who was there in the room when Meredith was murdered?' to which 38.8 per cent voted for Rudy, Amanda and Raffaele, 16.3 per cent for Rudy and Amanda and just 3.8 per cent for Rudy alone. The others were split between 'Rudy and the mysterious Italian man', and 'Rudy and one of his friends'.[14] Judging by this, and indeed the discussions which follow, the majority of the posters on here seem to favour Amanda's guilt, and often those who argue for her innocence are downvoted and ridiculed. This is echoed in the observations of Tom Kington, another journalist to cover the story who gave an interview in the 2022 documentary *Who Murdered Meredith Kercher?* After describing how they, the press, were drip fed information through a series of leaks, he remarks that he never really saw any evidence of his fellow journalists taking sides at the time, but that an 'army of bloggers' was watching everything he wrote and subsequently divided into two 'opposing armies'.[15] This seems to have certainly continued throughout the investigation, trial and beyond.

Four members of this subreddit kindly offered to help with the content of this book by answering a series of questions to try and ascertain what their motivation was in discussing the case, and to investigate what, if anything, sways their opinions. Whilst two of them were happy for the writer to publish their Reddit usernames, to protect their anonymity all four will be referred to by a pseudonym.

First though, one of the users whom we will call Charlie, a white male aged 25 from the USA, helped to clarify his thoughts on why the group seems unable to uphold genuine discussions about the evidence. He's often wondered why this sub in particular is so toxic and thinks:

> it's because the participants are so deeply divided and neither side really wants to meet in the middle. I love true crime and I have participated in many true crime subreddits, and Facebook groups and I don't often see people so emotionally invested in a case. I find this case fascinating and there are so many moving parts and loose ends so for that reason it can be interesting to discuss it with other people, but unfortunately, I think all the infighting sucks all the oxygen out of the room for real discussion.

It's clearly not just this sub where this happens, as he explains:

> I posted a guilty opinion on a true crime subreddit, and I was *descended* upon and I had something like fifty downvotes. It was wild to me since my comment was fairly mundane and in line with the court findings. And I had

> someone basically attack me with all of these pre-prepared defence points. They were very rude and condescending which is so perplexing to me.

The term 'keyboard warrior' to describe someone happy to be aggressive online while not having to deal with their nemesis face to face seems appropriate here as he explains: 'it's like this case has become political and there are many online warriors who are invested in maintaining the optics of her innocence', but that: 'when this case comes up in my real life or someone brings up the Netflix documentary, I usually find that people's opinions are much more balanced, and the majority are undecided or think she is guilty'. Despite this subreddit seeming to favour her guilt, he says that in his experience it 'contrasts so heavily with online true crime spaces', and explains away some of the perceived animosity towards the author during discussions as 'people with guilty opinions are also very sceptical of people who publish anything on the case because usually in the past there have been many inaccuracies and omissions reported in the media which tend to lean in favour of her innocence'.

The forums seem to show that most people are swayed in particular by one or two pieces of evidence, which prompted the first question to these users.

Is there one particular piece of evidence or behaviour that convinces you of Amanda's guilt or innocence?

Charlie confirms his belief in Amanda's involvement in the crime by explaining:

> I think the totality of the evidence proves her guilt, but the most compelling pieces of evidence for me are the

mixed DNA in blood traces in the bathroom where the RFU heights show that likely it is a mix of blood from both women (further reaffirmed by a Knox only blood spot), the Luminol prints, the falseness of Knox's alibi, and the staged break-in.

By contrast, a user whom we will call Scott, a 42-year-old male living in Los Angeles, CA, believes that Amanda is totally innocent of any involvement in the murder. His belief is based on the fact that:

no physical trace of Amanda Knox was found in the room where she is alleged to have murdered (or helped murder) Meredith Kercher. No DNA, no hair, no fingerprints, no handprints, no footprints, and no shoeprints. Meanwhile, Rudy Guede, the one person we know *was* in the room that night (by his own admission), left multiple traces of himself around, on, and inside the body of the murder victim.

He also very much believes that the lack of a logical motive is key, explaining that:

even if one goes so far as to credit Guede's explanation for his presence there that night, that Kercher invited him there and he tried to save her life as she bled to death, one is left arguing a conclusion which beggars belief. That two adults with no significant criminal background, propensity for violence, history of mental illness, or compelling motive, went into a fully furnished, 11' x 9" bedroom to carry out the assault, rape, and stabbing murder of a young woman, and did it without leaving a single unambiguous trace of themselves in the room (or of the crime on themselves). So far as I know, no coherent theory of the crime has ever been proposed which explains the absence of this evidence, and all suggestions positing a clean-up fail the laugh test. DNA and clean fingerprints are invisible in the first place, and any scrub down to eliminate bloody traces would've left clear evidence of the attempt itself, and no such evidence exists.

Another user whom we shall call Matteo is a 21-year-old male, living in Venice and Italian born. He, like Charlie, is convinced of Amanda's guilt.

Again, he says that there are 'several pieces of evidence that convince me of at least the presence of Amanda and Raffaele at the crime scene', and that following on from this, drawing inferences about their involvement is inevitable. These pieces of evidence are, he says:

> a bloody footprint incompatible with Rudy on the bathroom mat and other Luminol-revealed footprints revealed in the hallway; the scene in Romanelli's room (i.e., the absolute illogicality of Rudy climbing the wall and breaking into the cottage); a strong DNA profile belonging to Raffaele on the bra strap; the absence of a verifiable alibi for both of them (in fact, we know Raffaele offered at least five different alibis to different people in the aftermath of the murder); Amanda's confession (which I don't think fits nicely the pattern of coerced/false confessions) which casually happens right after her alibi is retracted by Raffaele.

He found it difficult to explain as English is not his first language, but essentially feels that although the strongest evidence against them is circumstantial, it is also 'clear and logical' and therefore, in his eyes, valid.

In terms of the break-in, he is sceptical because he thinks that first, Rudy wouldn't have broken into the cottage knowing that the 'foreign girls' wouldn't have gone home for the holidays and so would likely be in residence, and second, because there are 'no physical traces either on the exterior wall or on the grass (it rained on the night of the murder), and no shards of glass on the grass or on the exterior part of the window (as if the rock was thrown from the inside with the shutters closed).' He thinks that further proof is that Raffaele knew that 'nothing was stolen when he reported the alleged intrusion to the *Carabinieri*'. Lastly, Benjamin, a 24-year-old white male from Georgia, US, starts by explaining that he has 'ADHD, so I apologize if my mind is everywhere'. He has, by his own admission, not immersed himself in as much research as some of the others on the forum recently but is very definite in his belief that Amanda is guilty of a role in the murder. He firstly explains that it is a mixture of behaviour, and 'a plethora' of evidence, which causes him to think her guilty. With regards to her behaviour, he feels that 'her stories do not add up', despite her being potentially plausible as he says, 'it is easy to just listen to Amanda. She is non-charismatic and matter of fact.' In terms of evidence, he says that which 'incriminates the both of them would be the fact that the murder weapon was found in Raffaele's house', and also that they lied about 'both of them being together when Raffaele says he was not with Amanda the night it happened', alongside the eyewitness testimony casting doubt on their alibis.

With regards to Amanda's motive, he theorises that she was 'jealous because of the exposure Miranda [*sic*] was getting with the music video with Kristian,' (a reference to a music video for Kristian Leontiou in which Meredith appeared, made in England before she headed to Italy). Benjamin feels that this is 'related to her feeling second to Miranda [*sic*]. [Amanda] felt inferior, however she felt that she was inherently better, so it was driving her mad that she was having to settle for a "supporting role" in her life despite being the best, in her opinion.'

He goes on to say:

> I believe it was a cold, calculated murder by Amanda because of pure jealousy because of Miranda [*sic*]. Women compete with each other, it's biology. Amanda felt she was more traditionally the Eurocentric ideal of beauty with the benefits of being the 'American girl'. Miranda [*sic*] should have been no competition to her by her standards, but she felt inferior to her because she had 'everything'.

With reference to Benjamin's use of the name Miranda rather than Meredith – a mistake he made several times during the chat and even after it had been initially pointed out to him – he apologises, explaining that to him it's because 'Meredith doesn't exist here', whereas 'Amanda is actually like a C-list celebrity. She is a big deal here. If you said "Meredith Kercher" people would have NO clue what you are talking about at all.' While this is the opinion of just one person, it is telling, and shocking, nonetheless.

If there is a lack of evidence pointing to Amanda and Raffaele at the crime scene, according to Benjamin it's down to their attempted clean up, 'to make Rudy the fall guy'. At this point he's talking not only about the evidence that makes him think Amanda is guilty, but also that which, in his opinion, points towards Rudy's innocence. For example, he doesn't think 'that Rudy would leave a shit in the toilet on purpose, I truly believe he may have had his headphones in and could have been caught off guard OR he did participate, and Amanda is downplaying it', going so far as to say that he believes that 'there is almost more credibility for Raf and Amanda to be imprisoned over Rudy'.

So, does he think that Rudy's account of what happened is accurate? He seems to think so when he says that:

> This case screams for justice and it's been pushed to the side for years.
>
> I believe that Rudy, being a black man (coming from a Caucasian perspective), could have been shadowed in a sense that whiteness is usually more respected in law. I believe that Rudy was using the restroom when this occurred, and that he is innocent and the fall guy. When I examined the evidence, it would make no sense to leave DNA in the toilet. The most petty of criminals would know to flush their own toilet with their DNA in it.

However, he does also go on to suggest that 'there is a chance he is solo guilty, there's a chance he has nothing to do with it at all, and there's a chance that they all did it together'. Having agreed that any of these three scenarios might be possible, he suggests that if Rudy was involved, it was because he was 'really stupid and helped Amanda because he had some type of attractions towards her, because we've already talked about how Amanda lied about meeting Rudy prior in police interviews'. He doesn't believe Amanda when she says she only met Rudy briefly and asserts that they 'knew each other well', and despite insisting during interviews that she barely knew him, he claims that 'they were at a party together and he'd been at the house. I believe they all partied together, and Amanda downplayed her relation to Rudy.' He even says that 'she thought he was one of the most "beautiful black men" if I do recall. She knew him and knew him well. They partied together.'

When it comes down to it though, it seems that he is convinced, as was the court, that 'when Rudy was convicted the only way they could have said he could have committed it is WITH accomplice [sic]' and is therefore incredulous that Rudy was the only one of the three to be charged and ultimately found guilty.

In a final, slightly confused, summing up, he says: 'Rudy may not be completely innocent, or he may'. He goes on to claim that 'what I do know is that Amanda Knox IS guilty. Why [was] the murder weapon in Raffaele's apt? But to tie it together: Rudy probably [sic] innocent, of course there's a chance he's guilty.' He explains that he doesn't think Rudy was given as much opportunity to 'lay out and portray his perspective' as Amanda and Raffaele were, but ultimately decides that 'I don't think he's guilty.'

It's clear that all four hold strong views and are mostly confident in their stance, which leads nicely onto the second question.

Do they think it's fair to say that there might be room for doubt? If not, how do they account for someone disagreeing with their point of view so strongly? Why do they think they hold the opinions they do?

Charlie is very firm in his belief that the 'totality of the evidence leaves very little doubt and is more than sufficient to convict'. His thoughts on why people tend to disagree with his opinion of her guilt is that 'by and large they haven't read the court documents and Knox's Gogerty Marriott PR firm has helped to push the narrative that she was railroaded'. So essentially – no, there is no room for doubt.

Scott is more open to the fact that we can't all assume to be 100 per cent correct because:

> as a matter of basic intellectual honesty, unless one was in Kercher's bedroom (or in the presence of the accused) when the murder took place, I don't think they can claim to be 100 per cent certain they know who did (or did not) commit the crime. So, to that extent, I reserve some (small) level of doubt. But I remain extremely (and I'd say

justifiably) confident in my belief that Knox and Sollecito were wrongly accused and convicted.

Although he's coming at it from a different angle, it seems that he concurs with Charlie that people tend to disagree due to their slanted view of the case, albeit from the side of guilt, or innocence. As he explains, he:

> won't go so far as to psychoanalyze folks I've only ever interacted with in online forums, but I think I can theorize more broadly about it. For one thing, I only first looked into the case some years after it had been legally resolved, and all the evidence had been made public. From my understanding, the news media reporting on the Knox/Sollecito trial in the early years was largely slanted strongly against the accused. As a general rule, once people become invested and convinced of a given opinion, they have a difficult time changing their minds. So, it's possible some folks internalized their earliest impressions of the case and have yet to be dissuaded.

Benjamin agrees that 'there is room for doubt about what exactly happened [and the] context [in which it happened]', but asserts that 'there is no way that Amanda and Raffaele were not involved'. Going back to the evidence which he says supports this, he lists the following:

> The elderly couple that saw Amanda.
> The weapon found in Rudy's apartment.
> Lack of concern to call the police and Amanda taking the shower.
> The attempted clean up.
> Amanda's Victoria Secret escapade.

>Amanda's stone-cold matter of fact, narcissistic and slightly delusional yet obvious demeanour.
>Visibly lying during her interviews compared to police evidence?
>The lack of DNA in Amanda's own apartment.
>Filomena's bedroom…

Explaining his thoughts on why people hold the beliefs they do, he suggests that 'once you invest time into this case it does not stop. There are twists and turns beyond belief'. Benjamin is clearly no fan of Amanda, describing her recent 'desire to be a spokeswoman and "face"' as likely to 'give her away in a similar fashion as it did to Diane Downs'. His mention of Downs, a mother convicted of murdering one of her daughters and attempting to murder her other daughter, and son, in 1983, presumably refers to the perception of her inappropriate public behaviour. Diane appeared to relish the spotlight before her arrest and was interviewed, laughing and joking, several times before her final incarceration; ultimately, this behaviour played a large part in suspicion falling on her or, as Benjamin puts it, 'it gave her away'.

Again, Matteo agrees that 'there is obviously room for doubt, and this is evidenced by the fact that people heatedly debate the guilt of the three involved'. However, he goes on to say that 'I don't think the doubt is fully rational', explaining that 'the complete explanation for the evidence by innocenters [sic] (if one exists) is incredibly convoluted and therefore not very credible'. He sets much store in the findings of the trials, including the Marasca assertion that Amanda and Raffaele were present at the crime scene, explaining that 'after all, the trial is the most reliable process we have for reconstructing certain historical truths, and in the case of Amanda and Raffaele it was concluded at the very least that they were present at the crime scene, so I don't think there is a reasonable doubt about that'.

Do the users agree that some of the evidence in this case can be ambiguous and interpreted in different ways?

Scott agrees that it certainly can, depending on the circumstances explaining that:

> for example, if given more compelling physical evidence linking Knox to the scene of the crime, it would be easier to conclude that some of Knox's behaviours in the days following the murder were evidence of a disturbed young woman, in the grips of some serious psychological disorder perhaps making her prone to violence.

He goes on to make the point that of course, some people are happy to make that leap, even without the physical evidence to back it up.

> But examining this in a purely legalistic framework, it seems to me that acknowledging valid differences of opinion in how various pieces of evidence are interpreted ultimately forces us to conclude that Knox's and Sollecito's guilt is, at the very least, a matter of reasonable doubt.

> Where we truly run aground in discussing this case is in the chasm separating how much weight we tend to give various pieces of evidence in evaluating the central question of guilt and innocence. For me, the absence of physical evidence linking Knox and Sollecito to the crime scene is the hammer blow that ends the conversation. Any theory of the crime taking this into account while still hypothesizing Amanda's and Raffaele's guilt suffers from a huge complexity penalty, and rumours of cartwheels in police stations or lingerie shopping trips simply do not come close to overcoming it. But many who believe in their

guilt attempt to do just that – cobble together a jigsaw puzzle of innocuous details (always interpreted in the least charitable light) under the thesis that enough coincidences and social faux pas committed by a bright but admittedly sheltered 20-year-old woman will ultimately outweigh facts which overtly trespass on the laws of physics and chemistry.

Matteo seems not to agree in terms of physical evidence, but does concede that it can be 'true of certain elements of behavioural evidence that I find very weak, such as Amanda's cartwheels in the *Carabinieri* penitentiary'. This, he says, is because they have been explained by Amanda over and over during the years since the murder, and he admits that if this evidence is considered on its own and not in conjunction with the rest of the physical and biological evidence, they can 'seem to be as readable as she says'.

Charlie makes it very clear that he believes that evidence isn't necessarily interpreted in different ways so much as being specifically *mis*interpreted, especially 'without the proper background or scientific knowledge'. He uses as an example the 'negative TMB tests to claim the Luminol prints in the corridor and in Filomena's room cannot be blood, but this is incorrect since TMB is much less sensitive'.

Given that Amanda and Raffaele are no longer incarcerated, it might seem difficult to imagine the motivation of those who agree with her innocence in perpetuating discussions about the case, for those who think she is guilty it may be clearer cut. So, what are their motivations?

Charlie's answer is simple and succinct. 'My motivation in following the case is to help keep Meredith's memory alive and to hopefully make at least a few people more aware of the facts of the case.' Benjamin also keeps it short: His is 'to just help awaken society's collective consciousness. There are always monsters hidden in plain sight, if people could just open their eyes and do reading. Amanda is one.'

Of all of the users, Matteo has perhaps the most personal involvement in the case, being a native Italian. He explains that 'I was little when this happened, and I remember the Italian press treating it intensely. In 2016 I watched the Netflix documentary with curiosity, and it seemed ridiculous to me that anyone could seriously argue that Amanda was guilty.'

However, the tide turned when, a few years later, he 'discovered the trial transcripts and the case against Amanda and Raffaele seemed decidedly stronger than what was reported (especially in the American media).' In fact, he says that he 'felt mocked by the directors of the documentary'.

Scott goes into more detail by making the assertion that 'seven years after they were acquitted, the only people still driving the conversation about the case are those who remain convinced that Amanda Knox and Raffaele Sollecito are guilty'. So, if he thinks she is innocent, why is he joining the discussion? He explains that:

> I think their case offers a handy prism through which I can examine all the ways that people reason and think critically (and often fail to). I'm not drawn to the lurid details, nor to its implications on matters of criminal justice. I just take epistemology very seriously. Our brains aren't naturally built to solve mysteries like this. Learning to brandish Occam's Razor to its full effect takes practice, training, and a certain sort of brutal honesty with oneself, and frankly, time spent among those who do it badly can teach just as many lessons as time spent around those who do it well.

The final question in an attempt to establish quite what the outcome of the continual arguments is hoped to be, asks what would they like to see happen in an ideal world. Do they think justice has been done and if not, what would their ideal outcome be?

Benjamin is very adamant that in his opinion, justice has not been served. Again, citing the influence of her PR team he believes that 'Amanda should be pressed on what happened and I think the media should quit manipulating in her favour. I think she is a killer and should be in prison.'

Charlie is more measured, and explains that 'in an ideal world, I would like to see investigative methods become more advanced, the public to have more respect and deference for the justice system, and for courts to be more impervious to external influences'. His stance here makes sense, given his firm belief in the efficacy of the legal system in placing Amanda and Raffaele at the scene of the crime. Charlie is also, apparently, planning to study law in the real world which may also go some way to explaining his interest in the case.

Interestingly, Matteo feels that 'although to this day [Rudy] does not fully admit to having contributed to Meredith's death', he is 'the only one of the three who has paid his time and showed the slightest repentance for what he did'. So, although he believes him to have had a hand in the murder, his view of him is surprisingly sensitive. With regards to Amanda and Raffaele however, they 'should have admitted responsibility and faced some fifteen years in prison in Italy'.

Lastly, Scott laments that 'if two people spent a combined eight years in prison, and another seven in a protracted legal battle, all for a crime they almost certainly did not commit, I can't suggest with a straight face that "justice was done."' Even though he says the courts eventually reached the right decision, he describes the case as 'a colossal failure of rationality and Italian jurisprudence', so the result 'can't possibly be a satisfying standard for anyone who has an interest in seeing the Italian criminal justice system functioning properly'.

Here he also mentions the Kercher family, and what they have had to deal with over the years. As he explains, 'whoever is responsible for Meredith's death walks free today, while all those accused deny their involvement', and therefore, although he may be wrong, he finds it 'difficult to imagine that, in the final analysis, the Kerchers feel justice was served'. Ultimately, he says:

> at this point, the ideal outcome would be for Rudy Guede to finally admit his role as the sole person responsible for killing Meredith Kercher, and to express sincere remorse for it. I believe in second chances, and I wouldn't want to spend the rest of my life being judged as a monster because of a horrific crime I committed before I had even turned 21. Some people will obviously never forgive him, but this is about the ideal outcome, not the most likely one.

But really, is all of this discussion necessary, or ultimately futile? In Scott's opinion:

> Speaking even more broadly now – the human brain has not evolved to be especially good at making rational judgments about the world – not when given time to evaluate multiple data points, laced with intermittent information gaps, and in a sometimes-complex arrangement. When we were cavemen foraging for food in the wilderness, and we heard a tree branch snap behind us – *that's* what our brains were built for – telling us to assume we were about to be some predator's next meal, and to start running. But start throwing data at us, asking to discern what's true and what's not, expecting us to accurately gauge the relative

importance of various bits of information, throw in some Dunning–Kruger effect (among any number of other cognitive biases), and you start to wonder how we ever get anything right.

His reference to the Dunning–Kruger effect describes a study around self-awareness of our own abilities, and a tendency for those with the lowest ability or knowledge in a given area to overestimate how well they will perform. Conversely, those with a greater ability tend to underestimate their capabilities. In simple terms, the less knowledge a person has, the greater their confidence in their ability; or put even more simply – they are delusional in their self-awareness. He goes on to say:

Scientific advancements often make solving mysteries like the tragic (but altogether typical) murder of Meredith Kercher a matter of some routine. But give the average person too much information and too much time to think about it, and they are liable to outthink themselves. Like a riddle which, when first posed, seems to demand hours of ceaseless contemplation – and then you hear the solution and you realize the answer could hardly have been any simpler, and you walked right past it.[16]

More Questions than Answers

Inevitably, several documentaries have been made about this case and in recent years during the upturn in their popularity it has become a staple for several true crime podcasts. In contrast to the detailed and somewhat organic arguments online, these by their very nature tend to simply tell the story of the case, albeit from various perspectives and sometimes, with varying degrees of truth.

It's fascinating to look at some of these documentaries from the perspective of when they were made, with the first being aired on 17 April 2008, well before the first trial was underway and in fact, even before the official report on the cause of Meredith's death was released on 19 April the same year. Entitled *Sex, Lies and the Murder of Meredith Kercher*, it is inevitably lacking in detail given that, at this point, there were still six months to go until Rudy's fast track trial, and nine months until the start of Amanda and Raffaele's trial. Forebodingly, given the events over the next seven years, the voiceover asks the question: 'does anyone really know what happened the night Meredith died?'

Initially, it makes much of Amanda's behaviour following the discovery of Meredith's body, and her false accusation against Patrick, who is interviewed for this documentary and states his opinion that 'Amanda accused me because I am black', and that 'what she did was not good'. The line here is that Amanda accused Patrick, and then simply changed her story. The implication that she may have been coerced is not mentioned at all at this stage.

Already though, the criticism of Amanda's behaviour is key, with students from the university explaining how odd they thought it that she had turned up to lectures on the Monday after the murder, seeming not shocked, but simply sad, and Pisco Alessi, the owner of the Merlin Pub, expressing his concern that it 'seemed completely wrong' that Amanda and Raffaele were seen kissing after the body had been discovered. As they would have been prominent in the press at the time, inevitably the pictures of Amanda straddling a machine gun, Raffaele wrapped up in bandages holding a cleaver, video footage of Amanda talking drunkenly, reference to a story about rape she had written in college, and all of the 'Foxy Knoxy' headlines are shown repeatedly.

The voiceover at one point does admit that 'of course, there is no real evidence available yet', so consequently, it leans heavily on speculation. Meo Ponte, the crime correspondent at *La Repubblica*, explains that we still don't know what happened and that 'it's a mystery how and why she was killed'. He does bring in Professor Carlo Torre, who would testify for Amanda at trial, who believes the cause of death to be her major neck wound and inhalation of blood, and during a bizarre reconstruction with a poor female volunteer, aims to show that he believes the 'seizing and holding happened before the stabbing', and that it is difficult to imagine more than one person taking part. Furthermore, Professor Francesco Bruno puts forward his conclusion that Rudy acted alone, going so far as to suggest that it might have been an accident, with Rudy 'finishing the job off' by stabbing Meredith in the neck.

Playing on the perceived salaciousness of the case it sets the backdrop of Perugia as 'Dante by day and inferno by night', describing the defendants as becoming overnight celebrities; one Professor Franco Ferrarotti explains that in his opinion, when students live away from home, they are prone to 'explode', and that once in a while, as a result, things can go horribly wrong. Specifically, he says, he believes that due to this 'explosion', the characters ended up in a group sex activity which suddenly got out of control, perhaps even implying that Meredith was complicit.

Building up the tension, the film describes Amanda and Meredith's strained relationship, referencing the former bringing men home to the cottage and failing to do her share of the cleaning, specifying that Meredith had criticised her because of the men and not cleaning the house.

Several times, although they do cover themselves by explaining that as yet none of this 'evidence' is substantiated, they reveal evidence: Amanda had been seen washing clothes with an African man, there was CCTV footage of her entering the cottage and that neighbours had seen two people running away from the scene of the crime.

And then the 'aha' moment happens, revealing infamous video footage, unearthed during the investigation but uploaded to YouTube less than a year before the murder, of Rudy pretending to be a vampire and exclaiming to his viewers that he wants 'to suck your blood'. From then on in, some doubt starts to be cast on the narrative; they reveal that the bra clasp appears to have been contaminated and explain that, if true, 'evidence against Sollecito will be seriously undermined'. However, new evidence is now starting to emerge: were two knives used? Was Meredith drunk when she died or were the results faulty? Who did the mixed blood belong to? Interestingly, this is all told among accusations of confirmation bias on the part of investigators, and crumbling evidence against Amanda and Raffaele leading to a potential reprieve.

Showing a hopeful foreshadowing of her forthcoming acquittal, Amanda's parents explain that they 'just have to hope [the police] will release her', alongside Father Saulo Scarabattoli, her confidante in prison's description of Amanda as 'usually calm'. While the final voiceover rather optimistically states that 'Perugia is getting back to being famous for its chocolates, rather than its murders', it is perhaps Bruno's observation which hits home in the light of the future press coverage: 'I think if Amanda had been ugly, this would not have happened.'

Chronologically, the next documentary to appear is an altogether different beast. Entitled *Knox on Trial*, it was released in 2013 following Amanda and Raffaele's first successful appeal but before their subsequent re-conviction during the Nencini trial. It's a dramatic affair which could probably have been condensed down into about half the length, but the overall premise is that two of Italy's top lawyers have been brought in to review the key evidence in the case and come to their own conclusion about the guilt or innocence of the pair. For the prosecution, they present Fulvia Guardascione, a lawyer specialising in domestic violence, medical negligence, human rights and extradition, and for the defence, Alexander Guttieres, a 'no nonsense' criminal litigator with thirty years' court experience.

The key questions this documentary plans to answer are:

- Could Rudy Guede have committed the murder on his own?
- How was the window at No. 7, Via della Pergola broken?
- How did Sollecito's DNA get onto Meredith's bra clasp?
- Did Knox or Sollecito leave a bloody footprint on the bathmat?
- Could the witness have heard footsteps on the stairs on the night of the murder?

In order to answer these questions, they walk among a constructed replica of the crime scene, to the exact scale and layout of a number of the rooms in the cottage. To answer the first question, they bring in black belt judo and jiu jitsu expert witness Eric Baskind, who first reconstructs an 'unexpected' attack by restraining his assistant, Juliette Page, in the life size replica of Meredith's room, in the first instance proving that she would not have been able to get away from a lone attacker. However, through another reconstruction they go on to prove that if he (i.e., the attacker) were to have a knife in one hand, she (the victim) is able to wriggle free. Their conclusion? Although one person 'could' have committed the attack on his own, it would have been much more difficult to do so.

In terms of the question of the break-in, and more specifically how the window in Filomena's room was broken, they introduce forensic glass specialist Greg Waite who reconstructs the action of a rock, of the same dimension and weight as that found at the crime scene, being thrown at a reconstruction of the window. A loud crash ensues, and he concludes that the fragments of glass which project far into the room 'seem to match very closely' with corresponding photos of the crime scene.

He follows this up with a test of what would happen if the rock were thrown from the inside, which results in huge quantities of glass being expelled outside, something which did not occur in reality. What he describes as the third and 'most crucial' test involves the phenomena of 'window bulge', where he explains how radial fractures from the moment of impact leave ridge marks and stress fractures, from which one can tell from which side the glass has been broken. It seems a pointless exercise, as for comparison he says that he would 'have wanted to look at' the radial fractures on the original window, which of course he is unable to do.

There is no answer as to whether there was glass on top of or under the clothes, but from the 'limited photos' the expert has seen, he concludes that the rock was more likely to have been thrown from the outside than from inside. Moving on from this but still on the subject of the break-in, the experts enlist Perugian climbing enthusiast Ricardo Panella to assess whether or not the wall could be scaled from the outside. He was able to do so easily with the shutters both open or closed, which may beg the question as to how the glass was broken through closed shutters, a question which was not answered, but confirms that, in his opinion, a potential burglar would need only to be 'tall and athletic' in order to gain access through the window, via the wall below.

For the all-important question of how Sollecito's DNA got onto Meredith's bra clasp, they introduce forensic ecologist and DNA profiler expert John Manlove who puts into practice a rather underwhelming test which involves shaking hands with the lawyers before then revealing that he had previously placed fluorescent powder on his hands, thus revealing the transfer of the powder to their hands under fluorescent light. The purpose of this was to show 'how easy it is for dust, and therefore DNA, to be transferred from one place to another simply by touch'. The conclusion for this section is simply that 'questions remain unanswered'.

So, on to the bloody footprint on the bathmat featuring forensic podiatrist Dr Sarah Reel, 'one of the world's top barefoot analysts'. She explains the difference between taking a suspect print from a standing and walking position and proves this by taking both examples from a volunteer, showing that the toe stem is only apparent when the print is taken from a walking stance, not the standing one. She concludes by explaining that there is very little to be interpreted from the print on the mat, given that only standing prints were taken of the suspects.

Lastly, local sound engineer Dr Giancarlo Strani is brought in to discuss the question of the witness who claims to have heard footsteps on the stairs on the night of the murder. In the actual house where this was said to have taken place, and using equipment usually used to monitor sound pollution, he records his assistant, wearing similar shoes to the suspect, running up and down the stairs, with the windows shut, as per the situation on the night of 1 November. The voiceover tells us that in doing this, 'he'll be able to judge if the sound from the stairs could really be heard'. During a slightly awkward moment, they suggest to the poor witness, in whose house they are carrying out the experiment, that in their opinion she's mistaken, despite her being adamant that she had, in fact, heard the sound that night. After taking a day to process the data, the conclusion was that

Strani had succeeded in recording and identifying the sound, albeit at a very low frequency and that, in his opinion, it would have been impossible for the witness to have heard anyone running up or down the exterior stairs on the night in question.

In the end, the whole programme seems, unfortunately, to have been a waste of time in terms of answering those five key questions, as the two lawyers discuss their findings over a very amicable coffee, lamenting that there is still lots of information missing, with gaps that need to be filled, and that they have, in the process of doing this, unearthed more questions than answers and that in their opinion the entire Italian legal system should be in the dock. In fact, their final conclusion is that 'the only thing certain in this case is that someone died'.

By complete contrast again, and perhaps the most viewed documentary about the case, is simply called *Amanda Knox* and was released on Netflix in 2016, after her final exoneration. Amanda plays a key part in this film, and kicks it off with a moving monologue:

> There are those who believe in my innocence. There are those who believe in my guilt. And if I am guilty, it means that I am the ultimate figure to fear. Because I am not the obvious one. But on the other hand, if I'm innocent, it means that everyone's vulnerable, and that's everyone's nightmare. Either I am a psychopath in sheep's clothing, or I am you.

It's very well put together, and typical of Netflix, with several key witnesses giving frank talking head interviews straight to camera and must be absolutely fascinating to watch for those who don't have any prior knowledge of the case. It takes on a real 'fly on the wall' feel, a journey through the eyes of the police, witnesses and suspects interspersed with vast amounts of original footage of press conferences and crime scene investigation, dramatically allowing us to witness the moment when the alleged murder weapon, the knife, is found in the drawer at Raffaele's apartment. It's rammed full of information and weaves through the story mostly chronologically, with the majority of its time taken up with the events surrounding the first trial, with the final quashed conviction in 2015 occurring only in the last ten minutes of the film. The happy ending. *Amanda Knox* does aim to show both sides of the story with equal weight given to interviews with several of the prosecutors, most significantly, Mignini, but ultimately it was made as a reaction to their acquittal with the clear narrative of the unfolding of events surrounding a wrongful conviction.

Mignini's interviews make much of the fact that he had decided on Amanda's guilt straight away, and in juxtaposing them with Amanda's version he is not shown in a particularly favourable light. They emphasise his supposedly arrogant nature while he remembers triumphantly, 'my colleagues complimenting me and saying that at this point, there is no hope for the two of them', following the DNA results from the bra clasp. Much is also made of his religious beliefs, as he explains that 'life ends with a final trial. A trial with no appeals,' with the implication that he knows Amanda and Raffaele are guilty, and that they should, and ultimately will, own their guilt before God.

Amanda is the star of this piece, staring unwaveringly into the camera and opening herself up to vulnerability, with the focus on her persecution by the media backed up by soundbites and clips of awkward and inappropriate questions being put to her by various interviewers, delving deeply into her personal and sexual relationships. She is undoubtedly compelling to watch, particularly when explaining what she says happened to her during her interrogation, and further explaining why her conviction was, but absolutely should not have been, based on her personality or behaviour:

There's no trace of me in the room where Meredith was murdered, and there's no reliable trace of Raffaele in the room where Meredith was murdered. But you're trying to find the answer in my eyes when the answer is right over there. You're looking at me. Why? These are my eyes. They're not objective evidence.

However, in what has become a recurring theme, she sometimes threatens her own reputation with an unfortunate turn of phrase here and there and can occasionally come across as selfish, particularly when she describes Meredith's death as 'brutal', and yet follows it up with her concerns that 'it could have happened to me'. While it could be argued that it's a valid point, it is, perhaps, tactless to voice it.

While Raffaele also appears, and Rudy and the Kercher family are clearly mentioned, they play second fiddle during this tale. Viewers are told in a written addendum at the end that Raffaele Sollecito now runs his own internet company in Bari, Italy, and also serves as a true crime expert for Italian television. Other than that, he is a bit player.

Who Murdered Meredith Kercher? first aired on 24 August 2022. Of all the documentaries made it appears to be focused on Meredith herself and is also probably the most balanced and least sensational in the way it relays the events of 2007 and beyond. Divided into two episodes, the first covers the first trial and conviction, and the second covers the subsequent appeals and everything else that followed in the wake. Meredith does remain the focus throughout, with the ongoing narrative being that she and her family are still waiting in vain for justice to be served. For the first time, her life back in Croydon seems to have been properly referenced, hearing from the vicar in her hometown, Rev. Canon Colin Luke Boswell, who oversaw her funeral which he described as needing to be a 'celebration of life'.

As the title would suggest, the makers are still looking for answers about the 'most controversial murder trial of the modern age', questions which remain unanswered because despite Rudy's conviction, the Italian courts never officially came up with a definitive answer as to what happened that night; releasing Amanda and Raffaele, they decreed, as a matter of law, that Rudy did not act alone. To many, this case has not been satisfactorily concluded. But would that conclusion come from Rudy admitting his sole guilt, or from Amanda and Raffaele being declared guilty?

Interestingly, and for what seems like the first time, there is an emphasis on Rudy, and not just on his convictions but on the man himself. In terms of his crime, his lawyer and advocate Walter Biscotti, who still vociferously maintains his innocence, shows absolutely no regret in insisting on a fast-track trial for Rudy; the resulting fact that he can never be called to testify in Amanda and Raffaele's case is probably an issue for them, but so be it, he says. His client comes first. Giving his insight into Rudy himself is Professor Claudio Mariani, who has worked with Rudy since his release and describes his as a 'very polite and respectful boy' who, he says, suffers from an 'acute distress disorder', explaining further that Rudy has been burdened with a strong sense of guilt that he was not able to save Meredith's life that night. He concludes by saying: 'I have no certainty about Rudy's innocence, but I have a lot of doubts about his guilt.' Although Rudy himself is not interviewed, footage of him integrating himself into society and being taken under Mariani's wing is fairly prominent.

To the contrary, the film also gives much airtime to those who find it unbelievable that Rudy was not made to testify at Amanda and Raffaele's trial, and furthermore that he was allowed to change his story on multiple occasions unchallenged. Kate Mansey particularly talks of her outrage that Rudy is allowed to walk around as a free man and that he has never been compelled to give the answers to the Kercher family that they so richly deserve. Kate, who was a senior reporter for the *Sunday Mirror* at the time of the case and is now assistant editor for the *Mail on Sunday*, happened to be the first to interview Raffaele on the day after the murder when she bumped into him quite by chance while looking for students to interview about the case. She asked for a photograph and, she recalls, had to ask him to retake it as he was 'smirking' or gently smiling in the first, not appropriate, she thought, for someone who had just discovered a body.

Journalist Nina Burleigh, author of *The Fatal Gift of Beauty* written in 2011 about the case, describes the whole investigation as 'drenched in misogyny', and laments the fact that although plenty of information about Rudy was widely available, as she herself interviewed him for her book, nobody else bothered to find it out as it was simply too boring for the 'online mob', with Amanda holding their interest much more. Ultimately, she says, 'Meredith was just killed by a man, like 99 per cent of women.'

Of course, the forensic evidence is covered again extensively with Professor Carla Vecchiotti, who had carried out the independent review, explaining her views of the flaws in the case and Manuela Comodi, the prosecutor who had been in charge of putting forward the forensic evidence in court recalling how appalled she had been by the successful appeal, again asserting that the defence should have been able to prove contamination rather than speculate that it may have been possible. Clearly, and perhaps understandably, this injustice still rankles with the prosecutor.

Steve Moore, a former FBI agent of twenty-five years and now friend and advocate of Amanda, is on hand to refute the forensic evidence totally. Explaining how he had initially learned of the case through his wife, who had watched a documentary and was convinced of her innocence, Steve says he told her that she should trust the prosecutors and challenged her that he could prove her guilty simply by reviewing the evidence his wife had seen. However, on investigation he changed his mind; it was impossible for the knife purported to be the murder weapon to have made the fatal wounds, he said. The evidence handling was atrocious; had he been in charge he would have bagged every knife in the drawer and taken them all away for testing. The crime scene, which should have been rich in evidence, was all ruined. Why didn't they take Meredith's handbag, which should have been a key piece of evidence, away with them on the first day, rather than leaving it in the cottage for forty-five days? In a rather more serious echo of the keyboard warriors who follow this case, Steve describes where his views have left him; with a following of haters, some of whom have attempted to try and track him down and in extreme cases, he says, he has received death threats.

Another expert appearing in the documentary who has provoked a similar reaction is Professor Greg Hampikian. He was not initially known to Amanda either, having first heard about the case via the British press and, like Steve Moore, the more he discovered the more incredulous he became that the case had ever made it to trial. His main issue is particularly with the DNA evidence on the knife, the fact that the sample was so small that the testing did not fall under international standards and has never been validated, certainly not to his satisfaction. He is laughingly cutting about the Italian procedures and processes and concludes that the sample was likely due to a contaminant or transfer mixed up in lab. As he puts it, DNA is very good at giving us an identity, but very bad at telling us how it got there.

It's worth pointing out that Steve Moore and Professor Greg Hampikian are both from the United States, and there exists a barely concealed undercurrent of tension between the US and Italy certainly throughout this documentary, if not the whole case. If Hampikian is contemptuous of the Italian forensic investigation, then Biscotti counters, if not directly but certainly to criticism of the Italian justice service by the Americans, with the scathing observation that 'this courthouse in 1308 housed the first faculty of law in Europe.

In America, in 1308 they were drawing buffalos in caves.' Donald Trump is even heard to wade in on the multinational debate in a soundbite from back in the days when Amanda was incarcerated (and before he became president), that 'the president should get involved' and that 'people should boycott Italy'.

Although Amanda is obviously mentioned a great deal during the course of this documentary, for once she is not the focus here. For the first time, interviews with Raffaele are much more prominent and Amanda does not appear, other than through audio snippets of her reading extracts from her book *Waiting to be Heard* to punctuate the narrative. She's dealt with sympathetically however, with Burleigh explaining that she thought Amanda had an 'exuberance and a lack of awareness which got her into trouble', and that she was treated dreadfully, with the media obsessed with her looks and clothes in court, seeing her as disrespectful as opposed to the 'pure and unsullied' victim.

Raffaele's role in this film seems to be to confirm how this whole experience has negatively changed his life, explaining that he continues to suffer discrimination to this day and is still haunted by the nightmare events. He is particularly, he says, still bitter about having to spend six months in solitary confinement while incarcerated for a crime he did not commit. He reiterates the mistakes that were made during the trial, the injustice of it all, the fact that the police refused to test the sperm sample discovered in Meredith's room, for example. And yet despite all this, sadly, Raffaele still comes across as ever so slightly insignificant. Perhaps it is because he or the documentary makers chose for him to be interviewed in stilted English when perhaps fluent, subtitled Italian may have painted him in a better light and allowed his story to flow.

This documentary ends in a rather ambiguous way, with Father Saulo Scarabattoli appearing once more, observing rather obscurely that 'we'll have to wait until we get to heaven to find out the truth'.

Interestingly, he is a lifelong friend of Mignini and has since the trials apparently fostered a 'remarkable dialogue between Mignini and Knox', which is alluded to as a face-to-face meeting but not witnessed on screen. Mignini asserts that his alleged persecution of Amanda was never about morality, it was always simply about her behaviour sparking his suspicion. While we hear Amanda's voice over describing herself as 'haunted by survivor's guilt', Mignini also talks about his suffering, that he was 'unfairly scapegoated' and that ultimately, he is not the monster that Amanda Knox thought him to be.

In the vast majority, the many podcasts dedicated to this case would wholeheartedly disagree. The podcast format is one that has emerged and blossomed over the past few years and is now incredibly popular, in the genre of true crime in particular. Numerous episodes concerning Amanda Knox have been created alongside, of course, her own offerings: *The Truth about True Crime with Amanda Knox* and *Labyrinths*, which she co-hosts with her husband Christopher Robinson.

But those podcasters who discuss the case now seem to be overwhelmingly in favour of Amanda's total innocence and most are in fact incredibly scathing about the whole Italian justice system, their methods of collecting forensic evidence and particularly, Mignini himself who is often ridiculed as an egomaniac who liked to think of himself as Sherlock Holmes (without, they say, the talent to back this fantasy up), and the overriding feeling among the various episodes is that he decided on a certain scenario as to what happened right at the beginning of the investigation, and shoehorned the evidence to fit his theory. It might be worth pointing out, however, that most of the podcast hosts originate from the US.

Almost all of the major episodes surrounding this case were recorded after the 2016 Netflix documentary came out, with the exception of two BBC Radio 4 episodes in 2014 and 2015. Therefore, and as becomes obvious, some of the episodes which take less of a 'deep dive' approach clearly use the documentary as their sole reference point. This is in complete contrast to many online forums where the tide seems to go in favour of Amanda's involvement in the case, and which use many varied sources for their information including, in some cases, the original trial transcripts in Italian. Of course, the audiences for these media are totally different. Those who watch documentaries or listen to podcasts tend to have a general interest in true crime and have either never heard of this particular case, or have a certain level of knowledge and want to know more. A true deep dive is not really possible in either of these cases, although some podcasts, for example one titled *Real Crime Profile*, did run a series of ten episodes on the case. Hosted by Jim Clemente, a former FBI profiler, Laura Richards, a criminal behavioural analyst, formerly of New Scotland Yard, and Lisa Zambetti, casting director for CBS's *Criminal Minds*, it was indeed a deep dive, but one which established right at the beginning that in their opinion, Amanda and Raffaele are totally innocent of all charges and the majority of the episodes focus on Rudy, the evidence, and Meredith.

As an aside, Jim and Laura were instrumental in the making of the controversial CBS documentary *The Case of: JonBenét Ramsey* in 2016. JonBenét was 6 years old when her body was discovered in the Ramsey family home in Boulder, Colorado on Boxing Day, 1996. She was found to have been murdered, and the case has arguably become one of the most famous unsolved cases of the twentieth century and beyond. Did an intruder kill JonBenét, as her family assert, or did her killer reside closer to home? This question has been hotly debated for over twenty-six years and their documentary put forward the theory that JonBenét's brother Burke was responsible for her death, and resulted in the channel being successfully sued by him. There's no suggestion of anything similar occurring as a result of their podcast about the Kercher case, although the presenters do allude to the fact that, in their opinion, the Kercher family have been misled by the Italian authorities and suggest that they would be perfectly willing to take their findings to the family in order to help them to understand the evidence. While arguably a well-meaning, if slightly condescending gesture, it seems odd to think that the Kercher family might, after everything that has happened, look to a podcast for answers.

There is a pattern which occurs during the one-off episodes about the case, perhaps inevitable given that most of them last for just an hour or so, to condense the story to fit the time frame and, inevitably, make mistakes or miss out vital information along the way. Through listening to just three or four single episodes several inconsistencies came up on a regular basis: the bra clasp discovered weeks after the murder was found in the living room, not the bedroom; the faeces in the toilet was found in the same bathroom as the one in which Amanda took a shower; Amanda and Meredith lived alone with no other flatmates, and already knew each other when they decided to move in together; the knife seized by police was found in Via della Pergola, not in Raffaele's house; Rudy Guede is a convicted rapist, and a Dutchman. While these may not have an overall impact on the case per se, it is in direct contrast to the minute and detailed investigation carried out by internet sleuths. It also goes some way to explain why aficionados of this case, from all sides of the argument, hold these episodes to little account and in some cases are completely contemptuous of them. After all, if they haven't bothered to find out which country Rudy Guede originates from, how can their listeners believe anything else they say?

Campaign of Confusion

It's clear, certainly from the forums and to a lesser extent the documentaries and podcasts which have been produced about the case, that everyone seems to hold extremely strong opinions on Amanda's personality, which begs the question as to whether they think they are qualified to diagnose the mental health issues of strangers. For many it seems that the answer is yes, as the forums are littered with quotes such as: 'all her acting jobs on interviews since then are the work of a psychopath or someone dissociative in severe denial lying to herself', or: 'I think blaming someone who she couldn't possibly know is the real killer is exactly what a psychopath who was the actual murderer would say.' It appears that Amanda cannot escape the armchair psychologists even if she's perceived as innocent, as one poster claims that, despite the fact that they 'don't feel like she did any of the murder [she] definitely has some sociopathic and narcissistic traits'.[1]

But what are these amateur diagnoses based on? A simple Google search asking, 'what makes someone a psychopath', turns up around 16,100,000 results including: 'what are the twenty traits of a psychopath', and a 'psychopathy checklist'. An article on the British Psychological Society website asks the question: 'what lies at the dark heart of psychopathy? Is it a lack of emotion and empathy, a willingness to manipulate others – or, perhaps, a failure to take responsibility for misdeeds?', and goes on to confirm that 'all of these traits, and many more, are viewed as aspects of a psychopathic personality'.[2] Perhaps the fact that this knowledge can be so easily obtained creates the illusion that any layman can recognise these traits in another (whether they be a friend or a complete stranger) and apply the diagnosis.

Going one step further, a quick search on YouTube also throws up a huge array of body language experts analysing interviews, interrogations and trials to give their opinion on the accused. They are fascinating to watch and one in particular, *The Behavior Panel*, has analysed more than 100 people including JonBenét's brother Burke Ramsey, Jodi Arias, who was convicted of brutally murdering her on/off boyfriend but steadfastly maintains her innocence against all evidence to the contrary and, of course, Amanda Knox. At the time of writing, the channel has 667,000 subscribers and is hosted by a panel consisting of Mark Bowden, Greg Hartley, Chase Hughes and Scott Rouse who, in contrast to most of their viewers, are all experts in their field. Mark is a communication coach and expert in human behaviour and body language, Greg is former interrogator and resistance to interrogation instructor, Chase is a retired US military intelligence trainer and bestselling author on behaviour tactics, and Scott is a body language expert and analyst who trains law enforcement and the military. Between the four panel members they have racked up more than 20,000 hours of experience in their fields.[3]

In a two-part analysis posted in 2020 entitled *Is she really innocent?*, the panel analyse Amanda's facial expressions, body language and speech for around two-and-a-half hours before drawing their conclusions, but are very clear about the fact that they do not take a view on her guilt or innocence in terms of the crime of murder. As Chase puts it, they are 'not the forensics panel', and what they do is certainly aimed at being entertaining and educational but is absolutely not a speculation as to whether or not they think that Amanda Knox is guilty of murdering Meredith Kercher. The panel are also clear that there is no rehearsal involved in their analysis; they each watch the chosen videos separately and individually form their own opinions purely on what they are witnessing during the interview. In fact, at least one of the panel members, Mark, says he has no prior knowledge of the case at all so in theory is not influenced by any media bias.

In an indication of how widely discussed the case is among the general public though, at the time of writing, these two episodes together attracted almost 12,000 comments on the opinions of the experts. And put bluntly, what the panel see is a 'chaotic mess', and what Scott describes as Amanda's 'campaign of confusion', but with the very clear message at the end of the analysis: that they are not saying whether or not she is guilty, just whether, in their opinion, she's telling the truth. And the conclusion? That she has 'guilty knowledge', but to the question of if she's guilty of a crime? No idea.

These conclusions are reached through analysing several aspects of the interview, which focuses solely on her recounting the events surrounding her arrival at the cottage on the morning of 2 November and the subsequent discovery of Meredith's body, including their thoughts on the actions as she describes them taking place, the language she uses while describing certain occurrences, and her body language (or more specifically her facial expressions) when discussing key points in the story.

First though, Greg's initial reaction to her demeanour is that he understands 'why investigators chased her like she was running', with the opinion that the whole interview is loaded with red flags which might send an interrogator down the path of thinking she's guilty. In terms of how she reacted to the discovery of the crime scene, for example, they wonder why on earth she wouldn't flush the toilet when she saw the faeces in it? A natural reaction, they say, would be to immediately flush it away. And why did she continue about her business and not call out to find out who was or was not there? They point out that she seems more concerned about the faeces in the toilet than the blood, and Scott describes Raffaele as a 'wuss' for not managing to kick the door down, indicating perhaps that they didn't put as much effort into finding out what was going on as they could have.

They do discuss her facial expressions in a fair amount of detail; for example, they see a faint smile when she says the word 'murdered', and it's suggested that this is what's known as a 'smile of fear'. Is her eye contact normal? Does she show a 'micro expression' of disgust when talking about the faeces in the toilet? Does the nod and shake of her head, her eyebrows knitting to show confusion begin to reveal to us her facial patterns? They see eye rolls, a pushing out of the tongue which either shows distaste or is interpreted as a grooming gesture, and an eye movement to the left, indicating that she is having an internal conversation with herself.

But what seems to make up the majority of this analysis is the way in which Amanda says things, the language she uses and how she describes events, which has already been alluded to in her erratic email home to Seattle on 4 November and her written statements to the police. Essentially, they conclude that aspects of what she is saying to the interviewer are not truthful in terms of the way she relays her version of events; Mark suggests that she had already constructed the story in her head and that hers is a 'very well thought out' way of telling it, indicating that the structure of her storytelling means that she is aware that objections are likely to be made regarding some parts of the story, and that she must therefore pre-empt them, an example being that she freely mentions grabbing a mop as, as Mark explains it, the mop had become a potential issue for her within the story she is telling.

This is where the apparent 'campaign of confusion' comes in as the panel are interested in her repeated use of the words 'strange' and 'I remember', her conflicting assertion that she continually could not understand what was going on and yet then suddenly switch to relaying minute details about the case. According to them, the feeling she portrays is that while everyone else was alarmed, she wants everyone to understand that she was simply confused or, at times, creeped out. Other theories are put forward, among them the apparent tendency for murderers to return to the scene of their crime accompanied by someone else so as to deflect blame, so of course her use of the term 'we found the body' when recounting this particular element of the story indicates a red flag to them. They even get down to the minutiae of a pronoun shift during her narrative indicating possible deception.

Lastly though, a recurring theme in their videos when trying to ascertain whether or not a person is lying, is coming up with a 'percentage of truth' pertaining to what percentage they feel that the person being interviewed is telling the truth. Between the two episodes Scott's conclusion is 'really low', between 20 and 25 per cent truthful. Greg pre-empts his by saying: 'maybe she just has the most unfortunate body language I've ever met', but comes up with a figure of between 15 and 25 per cent truthful. The percentage of truth test is apparently Chase's brainchild, and his conclusion is clear when he states: 'I would never pronounce that this young woman is guilty, but this story is not true. And I would stake my reputation on it.' He puts her truth rating at somewhere between 10 and 15 per cent. Mark is more reserved, and his opinion varies depending on which clip he is watching, claiming to be relatively indifferent to the first two but with his feeling reversed in the latter part of the interview. In part because of a 'double eye roll', he wavers between Amanda being 60 and 100 per cent untruthful. He does, however, counter this with the awareness that no one is really able to judge another person on such a small proportion of evidence.

In the end, the panel provide exactly what they set out to do, an interesting yet ultimately entertaining analysis. While they say that in working together yet independently, they can provide a rounded version of events, with the perspective of four sets of eyes looking at a situation from four different angles, and yet concluding that they all see the same thing it does beg the question: is it really possible to be able to assess one individual's body language without all other relevant information about the case to hand?

In contrast to *The Behavior Panel*, criminal profiler Pat Brown also analysed this case during a live stream on her YouTube channel *Profiling with Pat Brown* in 2021,[4] by looking into the evidence from the case rather than Amanda herself. According to her biography she has spent 'two decades analysing crimes for police departments and the media', and has appeared on various news channels in the US over 3,000 times. She uses her YouTube channel to analyse 'crimes, criminals and psychopaths', and even offers to teach law enforcement officers, criminal justice students or armchair profilers the art of profiling at *The Pat Brown School of Investigative Criminal Profiling* and in 2000, she opened *The Pat Brown Criminal Profiling Agency*. According to her website, she holds a master's degree in Criminal Justice from Boston University.

Pat stresses that she is very much aware of how contentious this story is and references several times the issues which come as part of the territory when discussing this case; if you put forward one opinion, you will automatically isolate those who don't agree with you and vice versa. She had, in fact, been avoiding this particular case 'like the plague' because, as she ruefully explains, it 'does not make you friends'.

Her approach is to try and distance herself from the emotive element of the case and put together a theory based on the facts as she sees them. First though, she clears the way by debunking the theory that all three together committed the crime. This was not the way it went down, she says, as first of all she finds it hard to imagine people of Amanda and Raffaele's background becoming friendly with a drifter like Rudy. She also asserts that the room is too small for this to have taken place, and that everyone would have been soaked in blood had they taken part together; she just 'cannot come up with three people in that room' taking part in a murder.

After much discussion, including the theory about Rudy climbing in through the window (she is dubious), the position of the bloody footprints (they show Rudy running away and not coming back), and Amanda's perceived image in the press as either a devil or an angel (she doesn't agree with either, but suggests that Amanda exhibits narcissistic traits), Pat eventually comes up with her own comprehensive theory as to Amanda's level of involvement in the murder.

While she prefaces this with a disclaimer that it may not be accurate, she explains her idea that Amanda initially let Rudy into the cottage that evening, perhaps for a drug deal of some description. At this point Meredith came home, caught them there together, and was unhappy about Rudy's presence. She doesn't go into details of how or why, but believes that Rudy ended up in Meredith's room, with Amanda in the kitchen, covering her ears to block out the sound of Meredith's screams. Essentially, she says that while Rudy killed Meredith, Amanda was cowering elsewhere in the vicinity, but not in the room where the murder took place. Rudy then flees the scene, at which point Amanda perhaps attempts to stem the bleeding with a towel before covering Meredith with the duvet. Of course, these actions mean that she must then go and wash the blood from herself in the bathroom.

The remainder is punctuated with disclaimers that she doesn't know for sure what happened, but that she does not think Raffaele was there at the time, but rather that Amanda went straight to his apartment to confess what had happened, and he duly accompanied her back to the cottage to assist with a bleach clean up, for no other reason than because he wanted to help her out. In answer to the question of why Amanda would cover this whole event up rather than, for example, calling the police, she goes back to the theory of Amanda showing some traits of a narcissistic personality; that because it's 'all about Amanda', then the motivation behind all of her following actions would be about trying to cover up her involvement, to avoid being carted off to prison, if only as an accessory.

Her theory stems from the fact that she finds Amanda deceptive, and she truly believes that Amanda did hear Meredith screaming that night, as per her statement given to the police. Therefore, she says, she was 'probably there, did see something and doesn't know what to do about it'. In a similar vein to *The Behavior Panel*, her eventual conclusion is that while she doesn't find her guilty of murder, she doesn't find her 'innocent of the event either'.

Whether or not any of these theories are correct, one thing appears to be true: that watching these types of analysis apparently gives some viewers (who are presumably not experts in body language analysis) the confidence to apply this second-hand knowledge themselves; one commenter on *The Behavior Panel* video asserts that '[Amanda is] clearly psychotic', before going on to confirm that this is at least their view based simply on reading about the case and watching her 'bizarre' interviews.

STORYTELLING

Disclaimer

None of the following scenarios is suggested as being the truth. They are simply an exercise in storytelling, confirming how, by adapting the evidence to fit a theory, presenting opinions as fact and changing the narrative language, opinions can very easily be swayed.

Ménage à trois

A party city. Drugs are available freely in the backstreets, hawked by undesirable locals to the swarms of students who descend on the town every year. Casual sex between two such foreigners is fleetingly witnessed down a dark alley, a common occurrence.

A young black immigrant inhabits this world, weaving seamlessly in the shadows hawking his wares, eyeing up the pretty foreign girls who have become his regular clients. Although he doesn't just peddle to the ladies; plenty of locals partake of his services, in particular one wealthy, spoiled Italian boy who is loafing around half-heartedly studying at the local university.

Nearby, a cottage, inhabited by two Italian lawyers and one respectable British student is descended upon by a brash American, hitting Italy right off a sex and drug fuelled journey and desperate to carry on the party. Her one-night stands carried out in a haze of pot are beginning to really piss off her flatmates. Leaving sex toys all over the bathroom, really? Can't she just keep it to herself? And while she's at it, would it hurt for her to clean up after herself once in a while?

Party night in town, and the party girl is on her own, snubbed by the group beginning to really tire of her embarrassing antics, especially now that she's fawning all over her latest conquest, none other than the spoiled Italian boy. Unfortunately for the party girl, he's happy to stay at home tonight. What can she do with herself now? She's already had a row with her boss and is under threat of being fired; flirting with guests and drinking the profits was apparently not in her job description. So, she parties on her own, scouting for men, smouldering resentment building as she contemplates the rest of those prudes. They just don't understand her.

Perhaps she should visit her dealer? He seems pretty into her, perhaps an ego boost is what she needs tonight, but what about the Italian boy? Maybe she should save that for when they can all get together. She's pretty sure they'd both be up for it and besides, surely two is better than one?

A late night is followed by a lazy day, but the party girl is getting increasingly frustrated. The Italian boy isn't cutting it on his own anymore, she's got an itch to scratch. The best way to deal with it is more sex, more pot, an afternoon in bed with the boyfriend. And then she gets the idea, but first she needs a plan. Her boss has just sent her a text telling her not to come into work, which gives her the perfect opportunity to set up her potential scapegoat with an ambiguous reply. She and the boyfriend turn off their phones – they definitely do not want to be traced tonight – and head for town to find their friend the drug dealer.

She already knows her boyfriend is looking for cheap thrills, why not her dealer too? She's got them both wrapped around her little finger, so the promise of some illicit experience is more than enough to tempt them to follow her to the cottage where she knows her prim flatmate is alone, probably studying. What can she do to test just how far these boys will go for her? She's pretty sure she knows, and she's willing to find out. Just hours later, her flatmate lies dead at the hands of her puppets; she tried to get her to go along for kicks, but she really wasn't having any of it.

And now, she thinks, they've got to get away with it. Ok, they may have been spotted coming and going, but she'll worry about that later. Drug boy disappears, back to the backstreet clubs, leaving behind him a wealth of evidence in his involvement in the murder. The party girl and boy are implicated too, but an idea comes to her. Clean up the traces they've left, and we can pin the whole thing on drug boy! He's even left a shit in the toilet. Perfect. There's no rush though, they'll take their time with that bit and head back in the morning to sort the rest out. The bare footprint left by the boyfriend on the bathroom shower mat might be an issue; they must remember to throw that in the washing machine before they've finished.

And so, they return, after a quick early visit to fetch cleaning supplies they set to it, mop in hand, even cleverly faking a break-in to deflect attention from them and are making pretty good progress until the police arrive. The police? Why are they here? They haven't even got round to that part of the plan yet. Quick thinking required; officer, it was like this when we arrived, can you help us? We can't find my flatmate anywhere…

A body discovered, a slip of the tongue about its position in the room, but never mind. The problem is, the party girl just can't help herself; she craves physical male contact and makes out with her boyfriend right there in front of the police, and it doesn't stop there; why not make out with him at the station too, and while she's at it she'll perform some pretty wild acrobatics in front of the male police officer. If they didn't hate her already, the victim's friends can barely look at her now, and the police are beginning to feel the same way. She couldn't even be bothered to go to the victim's memorial, choosing instead to buy some sexy underwear with the boyfriend in tow.

But they'll get her; she can't keep it up for long. One night they manage to get the boyfriend to crack; he was weak, it was always going to happen. She's been lying all along, but will she take defeat lying down? Of course not, she'll bring out the ace up her sleeve, and blame the whole thing on her wretched boss who happens to be black, just like drug boy. After all, she messaged him that night arranging to meet up with him, didn't she? That will show him.

Unfortunately, her best laid plans don't work; despite their cleaning, the police find the murder weapon with hers and the victim's DNA all over it, and the boyfriend's all over the victim's bra.

Damn. And not only that, but they've managed to find the runaway drug dealer. Will he spill the beans? Or will her attempt at deflecting attention to another black man be enough to keep his silence?

The court will decide. The boss is obviously let go, and the evidence is damning against them. Their DNA all over the cottage, witnesses left, right and centre placing them at the scene. They've seen through the web of lies about the phone calls they made that day in a frantic attempt to cover themselves after the *Polizia Postale* arrived. Why couldn't the drug dealer have got rid of those phones properly, as planned? If he had, this would never have happened.

Despite a half-hearted attempt by their defence, the boy and girl are found guilty. And really, did they ever expect to be believed? Who would walk into a house with its door wide open and take a shower surrounded by blood? Who wouldn't just call the police at the first sign of trouble? And more to the point, would an innocent person really accuse someone else of the crime just to take the heat off themselves? The drug dealer is tried separately and found guilty, and the judge confirms, in law, that he did not act alone. It's the end of the road for them now.

The problem is, despite all evidence to the contrary, they are eventually freed on a technicality. Small samples of DNA and a less than perfect crime scene investigation were all it took to throw in a nugget of doubt. But everyone knows what really happened; they may no longer be in prison, but under Italian law, they are most definitely guilty, free only to live their lives under a shadow of suspicion.

Innocent Bystander

This is a story that starts much like the last, but our drug dealer does not know the party girl that well. And far from being a drug dealer, he's a poor immigrant just trying to make his way in the world. Sure, he'll smoke the odd joint and have the odd drink, but who doesn't? He's made loads of friends around town, he's pretty hot at basketball and he does ok. While he doesn't know the party girl well, he's admired her from afar for sure, even told his friends that he'd like to 'do' her, but that's where it ends. He prefers the British flatmate and she, he thinks, is pretty into him too.

Party night in town, and he can't believe his luck bumping into the British flatmate at a party and later on at a club where they chat, and most definitely flirt. She's into him, he can tell that, and he is totally up for it. Not tonight though, maybe they're both just a little bit too drunk? He will play it smooth and cool and arrange to meet her the following night so they can take it easy and slow. He goes to bed happy, in anticipation of the date.

The following day he arrives as planned after grabbing himself a kebab as sustenance on the way; she lets him in to her cottage and the flirting continues, but not before she lets out to him her frustration about her inconsiderate and thieving flatmate. Three hundred euros of hers have gone missing, and she's pretty sure she knows who took them, no doubt to be used for more drugs, more partying. She's had enough.

They are reminded of the reason for his visit though, and one thing leads to another; things are getting pretty steamy but damn, no condoms. He's a smart boy, a respectful boy, so they will go no further tonight. And just as well, as suddenly the after effects of the kebab begin to make an appearance, and a dash to the nearby toilet just down the hall is required. Now this may take some time, so in go the headphones and he settles down to listen to some tunes on his iPod, hearing only vaguely in the background the sound of the doorbell ringing. He hears voices, he recognises the other female voice as the party girl. Why would she need to ring the doorbell to get into her own home? Of course, he thinks, maybe the British flatmate left her keys on the inside of the door? That's it, he definitely remembers that happening. Voices are slightly raised, but he doesn't want to get involved so he concentrates on the tunes.

A loud scream rips him from his reverie, and he rushes out of the bathroom, too anxious or scared to even flush the toilet behind him, hastily dressing himself as he heads down the corridor. He's greeted by the sight of a man heading towards him, clutching a knife in one hand. He thinks he might be the Italian boy he's seen with the party girl, but he's not sure. He is sure, though, that the silhouette he sees disappearing into the distance is hers. He's *sure* of it. The Italian boy is triumphant, exclaiming that 'I've found a black man!! Black man found; black man guilty!' before lunging forward with the knife, cutting our man's hands and then hastily fleeing the scene.

And the scene from which he was fleeing was horrific; our man discovers the British flatmate on the floor of her room, bleeding, near death. He panics, what should he do? His first thought is to try and stop the bleeding, so he grabs some nearby towels to stem the flow. It's no good though, he can see that. And now his fingerprints are everywhere. The panic rises, mixed with a morbid fear sparking flashbacks to his horrendous childhood. He can't be here; he can't get involved. With a heavy heart he runs, runs as far away as possible and hopes that this will all blow over, or at the very least, someone will believe him. When he leaves, there was no evidence of a break-in that he could see, no blood on the wall, the flatmate was fully dressed.

All he can assume, is that the fleeing pair came back to the cottage after they were sure that he was gone and finished what they had started.

Lone Predator

Full of promise, the beautiful university town nestled in the surrounding hills is the perfect backdrop for two students to head to for a year's study abroad: one, a bright intelligent British girl, and the other – also intelligent and full of life – from America. They find themselves drawn to a pretty cottage on the outskirts of town, let by two Italian lawyers; before long they are cocooned in a happy new world, navigating the day-to-day obstacles of living together: an unclean toilet here and there, and the odd uncomfortable moment following a sexual encounter the night before. No big deal.

The American girl is keen to broaden her horizons, she wants to experience life and tentatively experiences her first one-night stand on the journey there, continuing to find her feet and meet new people once she's settled in, dipping her toe again into the world of casual sex while being not at all sure that it's for her. Everyone else seems to be doing it, so why not her?

And then her world changes when she meets the shy, handsome local boy and sparks immediately fly. Finding common ground through several shared languages they click right off the bat; in that first glow of what they perceive as love, they share as much time as possible together comparing life experiences and smoking the odd joint. Everyone in the flat does it too, it's just normal for round here and adds to the sensory experience of living abroad.

The flatmates get along ok; they'll never be best of friends, but they socialise together for a bit before the British girl and her friends start to tire a little of the American girl's quirky personality; it's a bit too much for them, but they can just ignore it. They sometimes get together with the boys downstairs who introduce them to a local black immigrant who seems ok. He's mostly high and sometimes makes inappropriate comments but he seems harmless enough.

What they don't know is that he's well known around town, his reputation as a loafer and a burglar precedes him; he's been known to gain access to properties by throwing rocks at the windows before scaling the walls and helping himself to whatever he can find, including food from the fridge. He tends to make himself at home, they say.

He couldn't be further from their minds when they party the night away on Halloween, the British group in one place and the American heading over to have a drink with her boss at a local pub before becoming bored and heading home to a cosy night with her Italian boy. A lazy day follows, the girls giggle as they share stories of the night before, and again split later that day, the British girl to spend a quiet evening before heading home for an early night and the American girl, of course, heading back to her Italian boy again. Should she be at work that night? Damn, that's the last thing either of them want to do, they're sleepy from sex and pot and just want to chill. Ping. Text comes in from her boss with a reprieve; there's no need for her to come in on this quiet night. She replies 'great, see you later', and they both switch their phones off before enjoying a night of undisturbed peace.

That night, our burglar is on the prowl. Unable to sleep, he spies the cottage he's visited on previous occasions. Nobody will be in tonight, right? They're all out of town, but best to check. He hurls a rock at one of the windows and, when nobody appears to investigate the noise, he nimbly scales the wall and lets himself in. It's easy, he's used to this, after all. He makes himself at home, has a rummage around the room he entered in to see if he can find anything worth stealing and then heads to one of the other bedrooms where he finds 300 euros. Result! He pockets it, helping himself to a drink from the fridge before casually carrying on his search.

Suddenly, a kebab he'd eaten earlier starts to cause problems and he heads for the nearest toilet where he relieves himself while listening to some tunes on his iPod. So far, so good. But then, his plan starts to unravel when he hears the sickening sound of a key in the door, and someone entering the cottage. What can he do? He can't risk being caught here, risk making a sound by flushing. Slowly he pulls up his trousers and ventures out of the bathroom.

If he thinks he's going to just walk out of here, he has underestimated the British flatmate who he finds himself faced with. But now, while he thinks of it, why should he just walk out? He's always felt sexually attracted to her and something tells him to grasp this opportunity; he follows this urge with an attempt to sexually attack her, in all her vulnerability. Again though, he has underestimated her. She is a fighter, and before he knows it, he has gone too far and finds himself looking down at a dead body. Dead, at his hands.

There's nothing he can do now, what's done is done. He makes a vague attempt at a clear up; in the struggle one of his shoes has come off so he heads to the bathroom to try and sort himself out. But he's not thinking clearly; he grabs the euros and wallet from a nearby handbag along with two mobile phones (why go home empty handed?) and heads out, not before locking the bedroom door and pocketing the keys. He'll dispose of them somewhere later along with the knife he was carrying, nobody will ever find them. He'll do the same with the phones once he realises they will do him more harm than good and flings them into a nearby garden before heading off to a club to attempt to at least create a semblance of an alibi.

The next morning it hits him like a train, what he has done, and as is becoming a pattern for him, he once again panics. This time, he'll get himself further away, and head abroad.

In the meantime, the unsuspecting American is heading back to the cottage to find a bizarre set of circumstances. The front door is unlocked, and there are droplets of blood on the basin in the shower room. She takes a shower nonetheless, no big deal, but then spots what could be a footprint on the shower mat – and worse, unflushed faeces in the other bathroom. Freaked out and now terrified, she heads back to her Italian boy for comfort and advice. A flurry of confusion occurs; phone calls back and forth with one of her Italian flatmates and, almost the most confusing of all, the arrival of some police in possession of two phones, when they had only just called the emergency number. How could that be? And then the worst nightmare, the locked bedroom door is broken down to reveal the horrific scene.

Our American is a like a fish out of water, she endures interviews in a foreign language she has a mere working knowledge of, she's exhausted, terrified and alone and what's more everyone is starting to look at her strangely. She's still the same quirky girl she was before, but now that a body has been discovered her behaviour is suddenly suspicious to them. She just wants to find out what's going on, what she needs to do next, sort out the practicalities of where she's going to be sleeping while this investigation takes place.

And the nightmare continues. The questioning becomes more intense, and suddenly they are telling her that her boyfriend has withdrawn her alibi. And now, they are shouting at her, why did she arrange to meet her boss that evening? Is he involved? Did he kill her flatmate? She knows what happened, and if they need to hit her over the head to make her remember then so be it. Terrified, exhausted and starving, she finally crumbles and tells them, although in her heart she knows it is not true, that her boss did indeed kill her flatmate and she was there when it happened. And so, her fate is sealed.

What follows compounds the nightmare; her picture is splashed all over the newspapers with lurid tales of her sex life for all to see. The police claim to have found a murder weapon with her DNA on it. This cannot be. A flicker of hope when an immigrant is found and placed at the scene, and her boss is released. Surely now they will realise that what she admitted to was rubbish, the result of unrelenting pressure?

But no, what this is all leading up to is a trial at which she and her boyfriend are convicted of a murder they did not commit. It is unbelievable to her that a separate trial for the immigrant had confirmed that he had not acted alone; in the eyes of the law, she will forever be under suspicion even if she is acquitted. But there is no hope of that. Ok, she admits that sometimes she can't read the room and behaves in an odd way, but surely, they can't convict her on her behaviour. She kissed her boyfriend at the scene of the crime, they say. She went shopping for sexy underwear after the murder, they say. She turned cartwheels in front of the police in an outrageously narcissistic display, they say. She needed comfort, she needed clothes, she was trying to relax, she knows.

It seems that behaviour can indeed convict, as well as evidence which she and her team are convinced was contaminated and unreliable. And there she finds herself, in a foreign prison, for a crime she did not commit. After a relentless six years of appeal however, she is free. Rightfully acquitted after the investigator's shoddy handling of the evidence they claimed would convict her is unearthed, leaving absolutely no physical evidence of her at the crime scene, and absolutely no proof of a motive.

For those who say she is, in fact, still guilty under law following a ruling that the immigrant did not act alone, she says this: that ruling was the result of a confession borne of coercion following hours of unlawful, violent interrogation without the presence of a lawyer. And is therefore, frankly, wrong. She is completely innocent.

AMANDA

Does my name belong to me?

During one of the many documentaries made about this case, a journalist discusses what happens now that the trials are over, pondering that 'it's really a matter of what does [Amanda] do with this newfound fame? Does she write the book and move on with her life or does she then try to go on Dancing with the Stars? I mean, that's when we're really going to see what her motivations are.'[1]

Although there have been no reality TV appearances to date, Amanda continues to be a fairly prominent figure, certainly in the US. In what is viewed as either a brazen cashing-in on the murder of an innocent girl or an uplifting success story of triumph over adversity, Amanda is now happily married with a baby daughter and co-hosts a podcast called *Labyrinths* with her husband, Christopher Robinson, along with a solo podcast called *The Truth about True Crime with Amanda Knox*. She's active on Twitter, with her bio, at the time of writing, describing herself as 'Exoneree, journalist, author of NYT bestseller *Waiting to be Heard*.'[2]

Inevitably she, whether deliberately or inadvertently, continues to cause controversy. During the Covid pandemic a tweet encouraging her followers to 'call me Vaxy Knoxy', alongside a picture of herself proudly displaying her vaccination certificate was met with general disapproval, but more controversially, a tweet she made on the cusp of the US Election results in 2020 joked: 'Whatever happens, the next four years can't be as bad as that four-year study abroad I did in Italy, right?'

The overwhelming majority of the thousands of replies expressed disgust at the inappropriateness of the joke with comments ranging from: 'this is so tasteless. Someone is dead', to a picture of Meredith with the caption: 'This is the actual victim, Meredith Kercher. She went to study abroad and never returned. Remember her name. Remember her face.' And in what succinctly sums up this case, and Amanda herself, one reply simply reads 'Girl, I don't think you murdered your roommate, but a tweet like this makes me understand why people thought you did.'[3]

But what does Amanda think of the continued interest in this case?

A plethora of semi-fictional films have been produced in the years since the trials, the first being *Amanda Knox, Murder on Trial in Italy* made by Lifetime Pictures in 2011, which was 'based on a true story' and interspersed with real footage of contemporary news reports. Starring Hayden Panettiere as Amanda, it's a highly romanticised and simplified version of events, and while it implies that Rudy's story could be plausible, it ultimately implicates him as the sole perpetrator. The Kercher family are barely mentioned, bar a brief portrayal of Meredith's mother towards the end.

The film was aired despite opposition from not only Amanda but also Raffaele, and the Kercher family who, despite their obvious differences, all seemed to agree that the creation of this film was at the very least misjudged, and at worst totally inappropriate and certainly in very poor taste. Amanda sued Lifetime over the film, which she describes as 'terrible', as at the time of its release the court case was still in the process of appeal and the fictional portrayal of imaginary events could have been potentially damaging for the defence. While they were unsuccessful in putting a stop to the film, amendments were made, certainly after the 2013 appeal, and according to Amanda it resulted 'in them cutting a dream sequence where I was depicted as killing Meredith'.

By contrast, *The Face of an Angel*, based loosely on Barbie Nadeau's book *Angel Face* from 2010 comes at the story from an altogether different angle. The film, released in 2014, is a fictional account of a writer, Daniel, struggling to complete, or even begin, a commissioned screenplay for an upcoming film to be made about the murder of Elizabeth (Meredith) and the three suspects in the case, Jessica (Amanda), Joseph (Raffaele) and Carlo (Rudy), with Cedric (Patrick) already having been cleared. Joseph, Carlo and Cedric are barely mentioned, and even Jessica takes a back seat, although the press bestow the nickname of Jessica Rabbit on her, presumably in a nod to Amanda's Foxy Knoxy moniker. The story focuses on Daniel and his relationship with Simone, a character seemingly based on Nadeau herself, or certainly the author of the book from which the fictional film has sprung.

A parallel, often surreal story unfolds, with Daniel meeting a young English girl named Melanie who happens to work in a cocktail bar and can make a mean mojito, also perhaps in reference to Meredith's encounter with Patrick at Le Chic. She takes him to a party where he becomes sick while trying to keep up with the energetic drinking and pot smoking of the surrounding students. Set in Siena rather than Perugia, Daniel also crosses paths with Eduardo, who appears to mirror the real-life blogger Frank Sfarzo whose blog *Perugia Shock* followed the case closely in real time. Eduardo, however, claims to have witnessed the murder and is in fact concealing the murder weapon in a drawer in his house. Or is this all a drug induced dream of Daniel's, in which he fantasises stabbing his ex-wife in the back while she is making love with her new partner, or conjures up an image of Melanie about to eat his heart? The key players all appear, and several lurk in the background as extras; Nick Pisa and Barbie Nadeau herself to name but two appear as journalists hot on the trail of the story.

This film was lambasted by Amanda's supporters, among them author Candace Dempsey who wrote about the case in her book *Murder in Italy* in 2010. Although director Michael Winterbottom asserts that his film is not about Amanda's guilt or innocence, as he explains 'we are certainly not going to be saying "This person is innocent, or that person is guilty." But we will be asking, "is this system of justice fair?"' Dempsey describes it as 'prejudicial' and claims that the film portrays the character representing Amanda as sexually dominant and relentlessly guilty.

While these films blur fiction and reality, at least two completely fictional tales have also been made recently which, although they allude to having been influenced by the case, are by no means a simple retelling of the events in Perugia. *Stillwater*, starring Matt Damon and released in 2021 follows Bill, an oil-rig worker who heads to France in an attempt to help his daughter, Allison, who's been convicted of murdering her female lover, Lina, in their shared flat. There are of course parallels; at Allison's request, Bill attempts to find an elusive man named Akim, who she believes to be the real culprit, marginalised in France due to his ethnicity and the subject of blatant racism.

In contrast, *Showtrial*, as its name suggests, is a fictional five-part drama made by the BBC in 2021 which focuses very much on the outcome of a murder trial. While it doesn't officially specify Amanda as an influence, there are plenty of nods to the case: microscopic DNA, no trace of Talitha, the defendant, at the crime scene, an accusation by her male co-defendant that the murder happened as a result of a sex-game gone wrong, instigated by Talitha, a misogynistic trashing of Talitha's reputation and dissection of her sex life in the press and accusations against the police of shoehorning evidence to fit their theory. There is even a nod to some casual racism.

However, one of the key themes it explores is the inherent unlikability of the female defendant. Allison, in *Stillwater*, is also not a character that the audience warms to. And spoiler alert; both *Stillwater* and *Showtrial* end with either the release or acquittal of the main character. However, and here's where Amanda might take umbrage, racked with guilt after receiving a hero's welcome home, Allison confesses to her part in the murder at the end of *Stillwater*, and Talitha's ambiguous actions at the end of *Showtrial* leave the audience wondering if she did, after all, get away with murder.

Understandably, Amanda Knox is not a fan of either of these productions and makes her views on both abundantly clear on her Twitter feed, and in an accompanying article titled 'Who owns Amanda Knox?'[4]

First she asks the questions: 'Does my name belong to me? My face? What about my life? My story? Why does my name refer to events I had no hand in?' This is in specific reference to *Stillwater* which, according to Amanda, is described in a *Vanity Fair* article as '"loosely based" or "directly inspired by" the "Amanda Knox saga".'[5]

In response to the release of *Showtrial*, she tweets: 'It seems I can't go more than a month or two without waking up to find my name and trauma associated with yet another entertainment product. This time, the BBC series *Showtrial*.'[6]

Although the makers of *Showtrial* have never named Amanda's story as a direct influence, her opposition to both *Stillwater* and *Showtrial* appears not just to be her alleged portrayal, in an albeit indirect manner, but more the feeling of helplessness and frustration in the face of her name being used in reference to events which, she says, had nothing to do with her. In direct contrast to her 'saga', she implores: 'I would love nothing more than for people to refer to the events in Perugia as "The murder of Meredith Kercher by Rudy Guede", which would place me as the peripheral figure I should have been, the innocent roommate.' Her story, she says, is 'not about an American woman studying abroad "involved in some kind of sensational crime." It's about an American woman NOT involved in a sensational crime, and yet wrongfully convicted.' While this may be true, the controversial story of Amanda Knox must surely also feature the accusations, the allegations, the investigations and the opinions of those who sought to bring her to trial, alongside the refutations, otherwise it will forever remain one-dimensional.

While Amanda has forged a successful career, she appears to be fighting a constant battle against reminders of her past or insinuations and outright accusations of lying both directly through social media and through at times thinly veiled screenplays depicting her, albeit indirectly, as a sex-crazed killer. Her supporters will say that this is unutterably unfair; she is innocent, and she should now be left alone to live her life with every right to pursue a career in whichever field she chooses. Of course, the opposing viewpoint is that if she wants to be left alone, why doesn't she just disappear? Delete the Twitter account, fold the podcasts, and live a quiet life out of the spotlight.

Some of the responses to her Twitter thread confirm the position of many people, retaliating with, for example, the question: 'did they talk about how you tried to frame Patrick Lumumba for the murder? That was a very important real-life detail to me. You tried to profit off of falsely condemning him, yet you don't seem too upset about that,'[7] alongside: 'Girl just be thankful you were able to return home. You're drawing more attention to you yourself than the movie is. But it seems that's what you're looking for. More attention. I've never once seen you associated by name to the movie. Let it go and live your life.'[8] Another harsher response to the Showtrial thread reads: 'Don't you think this is a little self-narcissistic? Nobody is ever allowed to write anything that may even remotely remind people old enough to know who you are of what happened? The world doesn't revolve around you, no matter how much you want it to.'[9]

So perhaps here lies the rub. Raffaele and Rudy have disappeared into relative obscurity, a path made much easier by the fact that their part in this was always overshadowed by the press interest in 'Foxy Knoxy', and partly perhaps because they just want to put the whole sorry event behind them, something which the Kercher family are unable to do. Amanda's motivation might be perceived as more ambiguous. She has chosen a public-facing career and is active on social media, ensuring that she remains a public figure. She has had her conviction quashed by a court of law. She has every right in the world to use her voice and relative fame to campaign against unstable convictions, to describe herself as an exoneree, to write books about her story, to interview other exonerees on her podcast. And although she also has every right to feel aggrieved when fictional or inaccurate versions of her story pop up on screen, surely, if she remains in the public eye then it is almost certain that they will continue to do so with a morbid inevitability, and while she can continue to attempt to right perceived wrongs, she is powerless to stop it.

And indeed it seems that her story is still not over. Although not as widely reported as might be expected, in 2019, just four years after her acquittal, the European Court of Human Rights ruled that Italian authorities had violated her rights to a fair trial by failing to provide her with access to a lawyer or a translator during her interrogation in the early hours of 6 November 2007. They also reportedly found that the authorities had failed to investigate her complaints of sleep deprivation and being physically hit around the head.

In a Twitter thread on 13 October 2023 Amanda announced that 'I am on trial in Italy again… and this is a good thing' before going on to explain that the Court of Cassation have finally acknowledged the ruling, paving the way for her to appeal her *calunnia* conviction against Patrick Lumumba. So, perhaps, there is still another chapter left for Amanda by the end of which she is fully exonerated of all charges.

But will it really change anything? No matter the potential outcome of the appeal ultimately, when faced with newspaper headlines like the one in the *New York Post* on the day when Rudy Guede was released from prison which simply reads: 'Man who killed Amanda Knox's roommate freed on community service.'[10] she must be left in no doubt at all that no matter whether it is fair or not, this story always was, and will remain, all about her.

REFERENCES

Publications

Burleigh, N. 2011: *The Fatal Gift of Beauty. The trials of Amanda Knox*. Broadway.

Dempsey, C. 2010: *Murder in Italy. The shocking slaying of a British student, the accused American girl and an international scandal.* Penguin Group (USA) Inc.

Fischer, B. 2011: *Injustice in Perugia. A book detailing the wrongful conviction of Amanda Knox and Raffaele Sollecito.* CreateSpace Independent Publishing Platform.

Follain, J. 2011: *Death in Perugia; the definitive account of the Meredith Kercher Case from her murder to the Acquittal of Raffaele Sollecito and Amanda Knox*. Hodder & Stoughton.

Kercher, J. 2012: *Meredith; our daughter's murder, and the heartbreaking quest for the truth*. Hodder & Stoughton

King, G. 2010: *The Murder of Meredith Kercher.* John Blake Publishing Ltd.

Knox, A. 2013: *Waiting to be Heard; A Memoir*. Harper.

Nadeau, B. 2010: *Angel Face. The true story of student killer Amanda Knox.* Beast Books.

Russel, P., Johnson, G., & Garofano, L. 2009: *Darkness Descending. The murder of Meredith Kercher*. Pocket Books.

Sollecito, R. & Gumbel, A. 2012: *Honor Bound; my journey to hell and back with Amanda Knox.* Gallery Books.

Websites

Brown, P, 2015: Pat Brown Profiling https://www.patbrownprofiling.com/patbio.html (accessed 17 November 2022)

Debutante Renegade, 2022: Amanda Knox is Guilty! YouTube https://www.youtube.com/watch?v=jxY2hPCnVX8 (accessed 23 September 2022)

Guede, 2007: https://themurderofmeredithkercher.net/T-intercepts.html (accessed January to December 2022)

Hellman, 2011: https://themurderofmeredithkercher.net/T-motivations.html (accessed January to December 2022)

Hyatt, Unknown: https://www.hyattanalysis.com/about-hyatt-analysis/ (accessed April 2023)

Knox, 2007: https://themurderofmeredithkercher.net/T-writings.html (accessed January to December 2022)

Knox, A, 2021: Twitter https://twitter.com/amandaknox/status/1420871392266911746 (accessed 11 January 2023)

Knox, A, 2021a: Twitter https://twitter.com/amandaknox/status/1459684768518266889 (accessed 11 January 2023)

Marasca, 2015: https://themurderofmeredithkercher.net/T-motivations.html (accessed January to December 2022)

Massei, 2009: https://themurderofmeredithkercher.net/T-motivations.html (accessed January to December 2022)

Profiling with Pat Brown, 2021: Amanda Knox, Guilty or Innocent? YouTube https://www.youtube.com/watch?v=BgitW3AfZvY (accessed 17 November 2022)

The Behavior Panel, 2020: Amanda Knox – is she really innocent? YouTube. Part One https://www.youtube.com/watch?v=YYu6l7TQeLg Part Two https://www.youtube.com/watch?v=7DOkwE53hEQ&t=1981s (accessed 14 November 2022)

Unknown, Injustice in Perugia http://www.injusticeinperugia.org/index.html (accessed January to December 2022)

Unknown, True Justice, the Meredith Kercher Case http://truejustice.org/ee/index.php (accessed January to December 2022)

Various, r/amandaknox. Reddit https://www.reddit.com/r/amandaknox/ (accessed January to December 2022)

Documentaries and Films

Bate, P, 2008: *Sex, Lies and the Murder of Meredith Kercher* Cutting Edge.
Blackhurst, R & McGinn, B, 2016: *Amanda Knox* Netflix.
Dornhelm, R, 2011: *Amanda Knox: Murder on Trial in Italy* A&E.
Hayes, Z, 2021: *Showtrial* World Productions.
Cox, A, 2022: *The Murder of Meredith* Abacus Media.
Leosini, F, 2016: *Storie Maledette* Unknown.
McCarthy, T, 2021: *Stillwater* Entertainment One.
Thomas, J, 2013: *Knox on Trial* Barcroft Productions.
Unknown, 2022: *Who Murdered Meredith Kercher?* Paramount Plus.
Winterbottom, M, 2015: *The Face of an Angel* Soda Pictures Ltd.

Podcasts

Clemente, J. 2017: *Real Crime Profile* (various episodes).
Soo, S. 2021: *Rotten Mango, The Case of Amanda Knox.*
BBC Radio 4, 2015: *The Report, Murder of Meredith Kercher.*
Killer Queens: A True Crime Podcast. 2019: *Amanda Knox.* Episode 88.
Sinisterhood, 2019: *The Wrongful Conviction of Amanda Knox.* Episode 36.
Those Conspiracy Guys. 2017: *Amanda Knox.*

Online Articles

Appelo, T, 2014: *Amanda Knox Author Blasts 'Salacious' Trailer for 'Face of an Angel': 'I'm Shocked'*. www.hollywoodreporter.com/news/general-news/amanda-knox-author-blasts-salacious-677647/ (accessed 30 January 2023)

Burleigh, N, 2013: *The Amanda Knox Haters Society: How they learned to hate me too*. https://world.time.com/2013/03/29/the-amanda-knox-haters-society-how-they-learned-to-hate-me-too/#ixzz2s67KsOmP (accessed 30 January 2023)

Carey, S, 2022: *What happened to Amanda Knox's ex-boyfriend, Raffaele Sollecito?* www.nickiswift.com/361399/what-happened-to-amanda-knoxs-ex-boyfriend-raffaele-sollecito/ (accessed 30 January 2023)

Casad, B, Unknown: *Confirmation Bias*. https://www.britannica.com/science/confirmation-bias (accessed 17 April 2022)

Duncan, M, Unknown date: *What Not to Do When Your Roommate Is Murdered In Italy: Amanda Knox, Her "Strange" Behavior, and the Italian Legal System*. https://harvardjlg.com/2017/09/what-not-to-do-when-your-roommate-is-murdered-in-italy-amanda-knox-her-strange-behavior-and-the-italian-legal-system-by-martha-grace-duncan/ (accessed 30 January 2023)

Dyer, C, 2019: *Amanda Knox's ex-fiancé Raffaele Sollecito announces he is engaged again to his new girlfriend*. www.dailymail.co.uk/news/article-7837837/Amanda-Knoxs-ex-fiance-Raffaele-Sollecito-announces-engaged-new-girlfriend.html (accessed 30 January 2023)

Firth, N, 2008: *Chilling pictures of Meredith murder scene reveal apartment bloodbath horror*. www.dailymail.co.uk/news/

article-508528/Chilling-pictures-Meredith-murder-scene-reveal-apartment-bloodbath-horror.html (accessed 30 January 2023)

Gill, P, 2016: *Analysis and implications of the miscarriages of justice of Amanda Knox and Raffaele Sollecito.* www.sciencedirect.com/science/article/pii/S1872497316300333 (accessed 30 January 2023)

Gunter, J, 2011: *Daily Mail criticised over Amanda Knox guilty story.* www.journalism.co.uk/news/daily-mail-criticised-over-amanda-knox-guilty-story-/s2/a546216/ (accessed 30 January 2023)

Hopkins, S, 2015: *Is Raffaele Sollecito turning into Amanda Knox? Italian bears striking resemblance to his ex-girlfriend as he insists the pair had nothing to do with Meredith Kercher murder.* www.dailymail.co.uk/news/article-2942707/Is-Raffaele-Sollecito-turning-Amanda-Knox-Italian-bears-striking-resemblance-ex-girlfriend-insists-pair-Meredith-Kercher-murder.html (accessed 30 January 2023)

Hoyle, A, 2007: *I fired Foxy Knoxy for hitting on customers: Patrick Lumumba reveals why he was framed over Meredith's murder.* www.dailymail.co.uk/news/article-496218/I-fired-Foxy-Knoxy-hitting-customers-Patrick-Lumumba-reveals-framed-Merediths-murder.html (accessed 30 January 2023)

Knox, A, & Robinson, C: www.knoxrobinson.com (accessed 30 January 2023)

Knox, A, 2021: *Who Owns Amanda Knox?* www.theatlantic.com/ideas/archive/2021/07/amanda-knox-stillwater-matt-damon/619628/?utm_medium=social&utm_content=edit-promo&utm_source=twitter&utm_term=2021-07-31T10%3A00%3A57&utm_campaign=the-atlantic (accessed 30 January 2023)

Malone, A, 2007: *The wild, raunchy past of Foxy Knoxy.* www.dailymail.co.uk/femail/article-498853/The-wild-raunchy-past-Foxy-Knoxy.html (accessed 30 January 2023)

Molloy, T, 2011: *Amanda Knox's Lawyers Threaten to Sue Over Lifetime Movie.* www.thewrap.com/amanda-knoxs-lawyers-threaten-sue-over-hayden-panettiere-lifetime-movie-24510/ (accessed 30 January 2023)

Orr, D, 2015: *How can a feature film about Amanda Knox ring more true than the news?* www.theguardian.com/commentisfree/2015/mar/20/amanda-knox-face-of-an-angel (accessed 30 January 2023)

Parry, R, 2007: *Meredith murder flatmate changes story.* www.mirror.co.uk/news/uk-news/meredith-murder-flatmate-changes-story-520352 (accessed 30 January 2023)

Pisa, N, 2008: *Foxy Knoxy protests innocence and details her many lovers – and her fan-mail – in prison diary.* www.dailymail.co.uk/news/article-1029136/Foxy-Knoxy-protests-innocence-details-lovers--fan-mail--prison-diary.html (accessed 30 January 2023)

Pisa, N, & Hale, B. 2007: *Caught on camera: Foxy Knoxy at murder flat on night Meredith was killed.* www.dailymail.co.uk/news/article-493028/Caught-camera-Foxy-Knoxy-murder-flat-night-Meredith-killed.html (accessed 30 January 2023)

Pisa, N, 2007: *Meredith sex killing: Foxy Knoxy changes her story… again.* www.dailymail.co.uk/news/article-499082/Meredith-sex-killing-Foxy-Knoxy-changes-story--again.html (accessed 30 January 2023)

Unknown, 2008: *Secret diary reveals Foxy Knoxy was 'always thinking about sex'.* www.dailymail.co.uk/news/article-1090608/Secret-diary-reveals-Foxy-Knoxy-thinking-sex.html (accessed 30 January 2023)

Unknown, 2009: *After her Aids fears, Foxy Knoxy tells of police threat to jail her for 30 years over Meredith murder 'lies'.* www.dailymail.co.uk/news/article-1192548/I-feared-I-Aids-sex-seven-lovers-Foxy-Knoxy-takes-stand-Meredith-murder.html (accessed 30 January 2023)

Unknown, 2009: *Meredith Kercher murder accused turned cartwheels and performed the splits immediately after Meredith Kercher killing.* www.mirror.co.uk/news/uk-news/meredith-kercher-murder-accused-turned-379640 (accessed 30 January 2023)

Unknown, 2011: *Unarresting the Arrested: FBI Profiler John Douglas on Amanda Knox and Raffaele Sollecito.* www.groundreport.com/unarresting-the-arrestedfbi-profiler-john-douglas-on-amanda-knox-and-raffaele-sollecito/?fbclid=IwAR0BFpZdYxT_Dain_gEG7IEB5rt6OZYAiSfkvrkkhH9kYplmEodjWdY9GzY (accessed 30 January 2023)

Unknown, 2022: *Crime of Perugia, Rudy Guede's book on Meredith's death and the role of Amanda Knox and Sollecito.* https://news.italy24.press/trends/91044.html (accessed 30 January 2023)

Young, E, 2018: *Important differences discovered between US and Dutch psychopaths.* www.bps.org.uk/research-digest/important-differences-uncovered-between-us-and-dutch-psychopaths (accessed 30 January 2023)

Zennie, M, 2013: *'I wish I'd never met Amanda Knox': Raffaele Sollecito tells how his life has become 'hell' as he prepares to face trial again for murder of Meredith Kercher.* www.dailymail.co.uk/news/article-2442261/Amanda-Knox-Raffaele-Sollecito-says-wishes-hed-laid-eyes-her.html (accessed 30 January 2023)

Endnotes

Her Name is Meredith

1. Debutante Renegade, 2022
2. Reddit, 2022

You are completely wrong. The evidence is clear

1. Casad, B, Unknown

Convergence

1. Bate, 2008
2. Knox, 2013
3. Knox, 2013
4. Knox, 2013
5. Russell, 2009
6. Knox, 2013
7. Follain, 2011
8. Bate, 2008
9. Knox, 2013
10. Follain, 2011
11. Follain, 2011
12. Russell, 2009
13. Follain, 2011
14. Sollecito, 2012
15. Knox, 2013

Hallowtide

1. Knox, 2013

2. Sollecito, 2012
3. Follain, 2011
4. Nadeau, 2010
5. Nadeau, 2010
6. Follain, 2011
7. Follain, 2011
8. Knox, 2013
9. Nadeau, 2010
10. Follain, 2011
11. Follain, 2011
12. Follain, 2011

Discovery

1. Sollecito, 2012
2. Knox, 2013
3. Knox, 2013
4. Knox, 2013
5. Knox, 2013
6. Knox, 2013
7. Knox, 2013
8. Knox, 2013
9. Knox, 2013

It Begins

1. Follain, 2011
2. Follain 2011
3. Follain, 2011
4. Knox, 2013

Suspicion

1. Sollecito, 2012
2. Knox, 2013

3. Knox, 2013
4. Follain, 2011
5. Knox, 2013
6. Follain, 2011
7. Knox, 2007
8. Knox, 2007
9. Knox, 2007
10. Knox, 2013
11. Nadeau, 2010
12. Knox, 2013
13. Follain, 2011
14. Knox, 2013
15. The Mirror, 2009
16. Knox, 2013
17. Follain, 2011
18. Knox, 2013
19. Knox, 2013
20. Knox, 2013
21. Knox, 2013
22. Knox, 2013
23. Follain, 2011
24. Sollecito, 2012
25. Follain, 2011
26. Follain, 2011

One black man for another

1. Russell, 2009
2. Russell, 2009
3. Follain, 2011
4. Russell, 2009
5. Guede, 2007
6. Nadeau, 2010

7. Burleigh, 2011
8. Knox, 2013
9. Sollecito, 2012
10. Sollecito, 2012
11. Leosini, 2016
12. Knox, 2013
13. Knox, 2013

Heading for trial

1. Follain, 2011
2. Follain, 2011
3. Follain, 2011
4. Follain, 2011

George Clooney's Wife

1. Follain 2011
2. Leosini, 2016
3. Leosini, 2016
4. Leosini, 2016
5. Leosini, 2016
6. Leosini, 2016
7. Follain, 2011
8. Leosini, 2016
9. Sollecito, 2012
10. Russell, 2009
11. Dyer, 2019
12. Carey, 2022
13. Follain, 2011
14. Blackhurst, & McGinn, 2016
15. Pisa, 2008
16. Blackhurst & McGinn, 2016
17. Malone, 2007
18. Blackhurst & McGinn, 2016

The First Round

1. Follain, 2011

Probable Identity

1. Follain, 2011
2. Hellman, 2011
3. Hellman, 2011
4. Massei, 2009
5. Massei, 2009
6. Hellman, 2011
7. Massei, 2009
8. Hellman, 2011

Reasonable Doubt

1. Marasca, 2015
2. Marasca, 2015
3. Marasca, 2015
4. Marasca, 2015
5. Marasca, 2015

Arguing with strangers on the internet

1. Injusticeinperugia.org
2. Injusticeinperugia.org
3. Injusticeinperugia.org
4. Truejustice.org
5. Injusticeinperugia.org
6. Truejustice.org
7. Truejustice.org
8. hyattanalysis.com
9. Truejustice.org
10. Reddit
11. r/amandaknox

12. r/amandaknox
13. r/amandaknox
14. r/amandaknox
15. Unknown, 2022
16. r/amandaknox

Campaign of Confusion

1. r/amandaknox
2. Young, 2018
3. The Behavior Panel, 2020
4. Brown, P, Unknown

Does my name belong to me?

1. Blackhurst, & McGinn, 2016
2. Knox, 2021
3. Knox, 2021
4. Knox, 2021
5. Knox, 2021
6. Knox, 2021
7. Knox, 2021
8. Knox, 2021
9. Knox, 2021
10. Knox, 2021